Cotswolds

Author: Christopher Knowles
Verifier: Michael Buttler
Managing Editor: David Popey
Project Management: Bookwork Creative Associates Ltd
Designers: Liz Baldin of Bookwork and Andrew Milne
Picture Library Manager: Ian Little
Cartography provided by the Mapping Services Department of AA Publishing
Cartographic Editor: Geoff Chapman
Copy-editors: Marilynne Lanng of Bookwork and Pamela Stagg
Internal Repro and Image Manipulation: Marion Morris and Neil Smith
Production: Rachel Davis

Produced by AA Publishing
© AA Media Limited 2007
Reprinted 2008
Updated and revised 2010

Published by AA Publishing (a trading name of AA Media Limited, whose registered office is Fanum House, Basing View, Basingstoke, Hampshire RG21 4EA; registered number 06112600).

 This product includes mapping data licensed from the Ordnance Survey® with the permission of the Controller of Her Majesty's Stationery Office. © Crown Copyright 2011. All rights reserved. Licence number 100021153.

ISBN 978-0-7495-6685-2
ISBN 978-0-7495-6698-2 (SS)

A CIP catalogue record for this book is available from the British Library.

The contents of this book are believed correct at the time of printing. Nevertheless, the publishers cannot be held responsible for any errors or omissions or for changes in the details given in this book or for the consequences of any reliance on the information it provides. This does not affect your statutory rights. We have tried to ensure accuracy in this book, but things do change and we would be grateful if readers would advise us of any inaccuracies they may encounter.

We have taken all reasonable steps to ensure that the walks and cycle rides in this book are safe and achievable by people with a realistic level of fitness. However, all outdoor activities involve a degree of risk and the publishers accept no responsibility for any injuries caused to readers while following these walks and cycle rides. For more advice on walking and cycling in safety see pages 16–17.

Some of the walks and cycle routes may appear in other AA books.

Visit AA Publishing at theAA.com/shop

Printed and bound in China by C&C

A04393

CONTENTS

Welcome to the...

Cotswolds

INTRODUCTION

We think of the Cotswolds as a collection of beautiful villages with mellow stone buildings, dotted with fabulous churches and wealthy country houses, and all set in a gentle landscape of pretty streams. This is true, of course, but the Cotswolds is much more than that, and this book will reveal the wide variety the area has to offer.

The name comes from the ridge of oolitic limestone to the west of the region, between Bath and Chipping Campden, whose wolds roll away to the east, creating the landscape that makes up the Cotswolds. Not all of it is gentle rolling hills. The Stroud Valley is deep and narrow with fast-running streams. The area near the ridge has some steep hills and wonderful views, such as those from Broadway Tower, Birdlip Hill and Cleeve Hill.

Rivers give the area much of its character. On the west it is bounded by the Severn, the source of much former wealth and a busy river today. The Thames rises in the Cotswolds near Cheltenham, and many of the pretty rivers, such as the Churn, Windrush, Evenlode, Coln and Leach, that glitter through the area are tributaries of this river. Much of the countryside is farmland, often broken up with drystone walls – a characteristic rural feature of the area.

The Cotswolds has been a magnet for artists and craftsmen for centuries. Most famously, William Morris and many of the followers of the Arts and Crafts Movement came to live and work here. The Cotswold Woollen Weavers at Filkins, the group of artists and craftsmen at Bredon Hill and many others keep alive the ideals of quality workmanship and personal commitment espoused by the Arts and Crafts Movement.

The beautiful churches in the Cotswolds benefited not just from the exquisite work of the Arts and Crafts Movement, but also from the wealth that was generated from the wool trade in the 14th and 15th centuries, and the results are a delight to all those who visit them.

Yet it is the villages of the Cotswolds that give it its special appeal – their pretty cottages, well-kept gardens, charming pubs, local shops, quiet churches and village greens. No visit to the area would be complete without looking round Chipping Campden, the Slaughters, Bourton-on-the-Water and, of course, Broadway. The smaller, less famous villages can be just as rewarding, and many are described in the following pages.

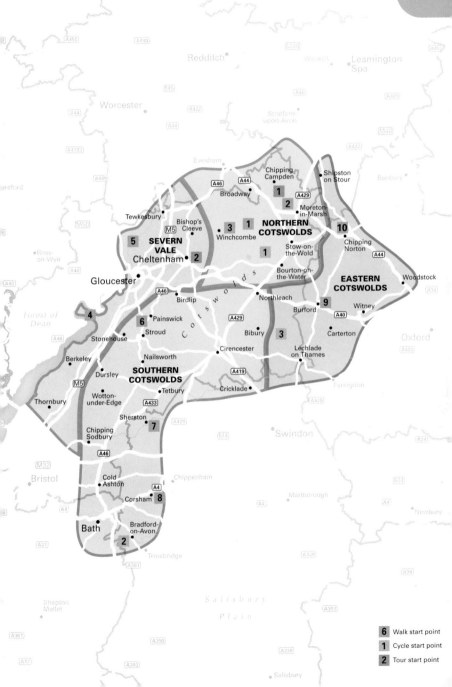

6 Walk start point

1 Cycle start point

2 Tour start point

Essential Sights

If you have little time and you want to sample the essence of the Cotswolds: See the views from the Cotswold edge, particularly from Leckhampton or Cleeve Hill or Uley Bury... Walk part of the Cotswold Way or along the Coln Valley... Visit Stanway House with its charming gatehouse... Climb Sandhurst Hill by the River Severn and look back across the vale... Enjoy afternoon tea at the Pump Rooms in Bath or a beer from the local Donnington brewery at the Mount Inn, Stanton... Experience the races at the Cheltenham Gold Cup... Discover the 'lost' Saxon chapel built by Earl Odda... Marvel at the world's greatest collection of waterfowl at Slimbridge... Visit the grand palace of Blenheim, a gift from Queen Anne to the Duke of Marlborough... Admire the church at Chipping Campden, perhaps the finest of the wool churches.

1 View from Cotswolds Edge
The wolds are an area of undulations that roll away from Cotswolds Edge. On the plateau and among its folds, villages built entirely out of gilded limestone and stone slate have changed only little since sheep covered the land lying between them.

2 Kelmscott Manor
Kelmscott Manor was home to William Morris for 25 years. From here, he led the Arts and Crafts Movement which used expert craftsmanship and good, solid materials to produce simple, classic items, such as furniture, glass and textiles.

3 Stow church
The Norman church of St Edward in Stow-on-the-Wold has two ancient yew trees framing its north door. Probably planted in the 17th or 18th century, the trees appear to have grown into the walls.

4 Slimbridge
This Wildfowl and Wetlands Trust property, covering 120 acres (48ha), attracts more varieties of wildfowl than any other similar site in the world. The property was founded by the ornithologist and conservationist Sir Peter Scott, who also co-founded the World Wildlife Fund.

5 Bourton-on-the-Water
Known for its bridges spanning the River Windrush, Bourton is a pretty village that has much to interest visitors.

6

7

6 Blenheim Palace
The home of the Dukes of Marlborough is an imposing property set in a magnificent estate of almost 12,350 acres (5,000ha). Visiting the palace and gardens will happily fill a day. The palace hosts special events throughout the year.

7 Hidcote Manor Garden
When Major Lawrence Johnston, the well-known horticulturalist, acquired Hidcote Manor in 1907, it consisted of only the house, a cedar tree and a number of beeches. He transformed the grounds and created an elaborate garden that is generally considered to be one of the most influential of the 20th century.

DAY ONE

For many people a weekend break or a long weekend is a popular way of spending their leisure time. These pages offer a loosely planned itinerary designed to ensure that you make the most of your time, whatever the weather, and see and enjoy the very best the area has to offer.

Friday Night

Spend your first night at St Michael's, in the village of Painswick. It is a superb restaurant with three lovely bedrooms, each beautifully furnished. Alternatively, in Cheltenham, the Hotel du Vin, Clarence Court and the Gorge all offer comfortable accommodation in a central location. In the evening enjoy a wander around Cheltenham, the 'Centre for the Cotswolds' and a town of considerable charm and elegance, its handsome, wide streets lined with Regency-style villas and terraces.

Saturday Morning

If it's raining return to Cheltenham and keep under cover in the Art Gallery and Museum and the Pittville Pump Room, which has an imaginative costume exhibition; after lunch go to Snowshill.

Head up the escarpment on to the wolds through Prestbury and over Cleeve Hill. Stop near Belas Knap, one of the best-preserved Neolithic barrows in the country, to enjoy the view across to Winchcombe. Then visit the town, its handsome church and Sudeley Castle and Gardens, one of England's most impressive historic houses with many royal connections; the entrance is down Vineyard Street.

After Sudeley take the byways east and north and don't miss Guiting Power, Naunton and Snowshill.

Saturday Lunch

For lunch The White Hart in Winchcombe is a lively pub with good food and a huge variety of wines. Alternatively, there are good village pubs in both Guiting Power and Ford.

Saturday Afternoon

Continue via Snowshill (only visit Snowshill Manor just as it opens, to avoid the crowds) to Chipping Campden and devote at least a couple of hours to exploring this wonderful village. Drive to Burford via Moreton-in-Marsh and Stow-on-the-Wold.

Saturday Night

The Bay Tree in Burford, dating back to Tudor times, is luxurious with comfortable four-poster beds that have never left the building. The Lamb is a less expensive and excellent alternative.

BATH

DAY TWO

Your second and final day starts with a pleasant walk to two of the charming villages in the Windrush Valley, before driving west to the medieval wool town of Cirencester, which is easily explored on foot. Round off your weekend in the Cotswolds with a visit to the Roman city of Bath.

Sunday Morning

If it is raining go straight to Bath with its many attractions, No 1 Royal Crescent, the Roman Baths and Pump Room and the Building of Bath Museum to name only a few.

If the weather is fine take a stroll east along the River Windrush to visit Widford church and Swinbrook village. Then drive to Cirencester via the A361 and the A417 through Fairford (the church here has some spectacular stained glass), or via the A40 and the B4425 through Bibury (picturesque but frequently crowded).

Cirencester, the most important of the Cotswold wool towns in the Middle Ages is most easily explored on foot and the Market Square is the most convenient place to begin a discovery of the town.

Sunday Lunch

The Swan at Swinbrook serves excellent food, whilst in Bibury, one of the most beautiful villages, the Catherine Wheel serves good food and has pretty gardens. In Cirencester itself there are inns on the Market Square near the church.

Sunday Afternoon

If time permits, a late afternoon visit to Bath can be recommended, as the tourists are beginning to disperse. One of the most magnificent towns in Europe, Bath is known chiefly for its Roman baths and for the elegance of its Georgian architecture.

To see another side of the Cotswolds, drive along the Golden Valley towards Stroud and then head south through Nailsworth to Tetbury, with its charming Georgian church and Market House.

Route facts

MINIMUM TIME The time stated for completing each route is the estimated minimum time that a reasonably fit family group of walkers or cyclists would take to complete the circuit. This does not allow for rest or refreshment stops.

OS MAP Each route is shown on a map. However, some detail is lost because of the restrictions imposed by scale, so for this reason, we recommend that you use the maps in conjunction with a more detailed Ordnance Survey map. The relevant map for each walk or cycle ride is listed.

START This indicates the start location and parking area. This is a six-figure grid reference prefixed by two letters showing which 62.5-mile (100km) square of the National Grid it refers to. You'll find more information on grid references on most Ordnance Survey maps.

CYCLE HIRE We list, within reason, the nearest cycle hire shop/centre.

❶ Here we highlight any potential difficulties or dangers along the cycle ride or walk. If a particular route is suitable for older, fitter children we say so here. Also, we give guidelines of a route's suitability for younger children, for example the symbol 8+ indicates that the route can probably be attempted by children aged 8 years and above.

Walks & Cycle Rides

Each walk and cycle ride has a panel giving information for the walker and cyclist, including the distance, terrain, nature of the paths, and where to park your car.

WALKING

All of the walks are suitable for families, but less experienced family groups, especially those with younger children, should try the shorter walks. Route finding is usually straightforward, but the maps are for guidance only and we recommend that you always take the relevant Ordnance Survey map with you.

Risks

Although each walk has been researched with a view to minimising any risks, no walk in the countryside can be considered to be completely free from risk. Walking in the outdoors will always require a degree of common sense and judgement to ensure that it is as safe as possible, especially for young children.

• Be particularly careful on cliff paths and in upland terrain, where the consequences of a slip can be serious.

• Remember to check tidal conditions before walking on the seashore.

• Some sections of route are by, or cross, busy roads.

Remember traffic is a danger even on minor country lanes.

• Be careful around farmyard machinery and livestock.

• Be prepared for the consequences of changes in the weather and check the forecast before you set out.

• Ensure the whole family is properly equipped, wearing suitable clothing and a good pair of boots or sturdy walking shoes. Take waterproof clothing with you and a torch if you are walking in the winter months.

• Remember the weather can change quickly at any time of the year, and in moorland and heathland areas, mist and fog can make route-finding much harder. In summer, take account of the heat and sun by wearing a hat, sunscreen and carrying enough water.

• On walks away from centres of population you should carry a mobile phone, whistle and, if possible, a survival bag. If you do have an accident requiring emergency services, make a note of your position as accurately as possible and dial 999 (112 on a mobile).

CYCLING

In devising the cycle rides in this guide, every effort has been made to use designated cycle paths, or to link them with quiet country lanes and waymarked byways and bridleways. In a few cases, some fairly busy B-roads have been used to join up with quieter routes.

Rules of the road

• Ride in single file on narrow and busy roads.
• Be alert, look and listen for traffic, especially on narrow lanes and blind bends and be extra careful when descending steep hills, as loose gravel or a poor road surface can lead to an accident.
• In wet weather make sure that you keep an appropriate distance between you and other riders.
• Make sure you indicate your intentions clearly.
• Brush up on *The Highway Code* before venturing out onto the road.

Off-road safety code of conduct

• Only ride where you know it is legal to do so. Cyclists are not allowed to cycle on public footpaths (yellow waymarkers). The only 'rights of way' open to cyclists are bridleways (blue markers) and unsurfaced tracks, known as byways, which are open to all traffic and waymarked in red.
• Canal tow paths: you need a permit to cycle on some stretches of tow path (www.waterscape.com). Remember that access paths can be steep and slippery so always push your bike under low bridges and by locks.
• Always yield to walkers and horses, giving adequate warning of your approach.
• Don't expect to cycle at high speeds.
• Keep to the main trail to avoid any unnecessary erosion to the area beside the trail and to prevent skidding, especially in wet weather conditions.
• Remember to follow the Country Code.

Preparing your bicycle

Check the wheels, tyres, brakes and cables. Lubricate hubs, pedals, gear mechanisms and cables. Make sure you have a pump, a bell, a rear rack to carry panniers and a set of lights.

Equipment

• A cycling helmet provides essential protection.
• Make sure you are visible to other road users, by wearing light-coloured or luminous clothing in daylight and sashes or reflective strips in failing light and darkness.
• Take extra clothes with you, depending on the season, and a wind/waterproof jacket.
• Carry a basic tool kit, a pump, a strong lock and a first aid kit.
• Always carry enough water for your outing.

Walk Map Legend

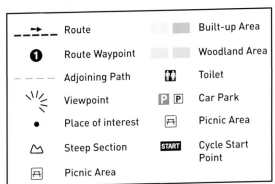

Route	Built-up Area
❶ Route Waypoint	Woodland Area
Adjoining Path	🚻 Toilet
Viewpoint	P P Car Park
• Place of interest	🏠 Picnic Area
⌒ Steep Section	START Cycle Start Point
🏠 Picnic Area	

Northern Cotswolds

Set in wide valleys run through with shallow streams, the northern Cotswold villages, such as Bourton-on-the-Water, the Slaughters and Stanton, are famously picturesque. Built using the local stone, they are the colour of honey, and many of these hamlets have barely changed since the time when the wool industry became the cloth industry and moved to the steeper southern valleys.

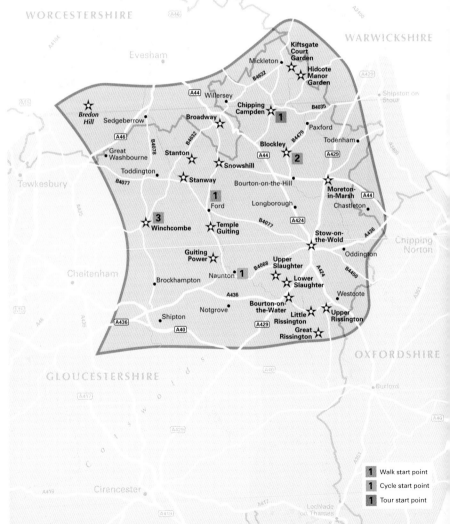

WORCESTERSHIRE

WARWICKSHIRE

Evesham

Mickleton

Kiftsgate Court Garden

Hidcote Manor Garden

Shipston on Stour

Willersey

Chipping Campden **1**

B4035

Bredon Hill

Sedgeberrow

Broadway

Paxford

Blockley **2**

Todenham

Great Washbourne

Stanton

Snowshill

Bourton-on-the-Hill

Moreton-in-Marsh

Toddington

Stanway

Longborough

Chastleton

Tewkesbury

Ford

Stow-on-the-Wold

Chipping Norton

3 Winchcombe

Temple Guiting

Oddington

Guiting Power

Upper Slaughter

Cheltenham

Brockhampton

Naunton **1**

Lower Slaughter

Westcote

Notgrove

Bourton-on-the-Water

Shipton

Little Rissington

Upper Rissington

Great Rissington

OXFORDSHIRE

GLOUCESTERSHIRE

Burford

Cirencester

Lechlade on Thames

1 Walk start point

1 Cycle start point

1 Tour start point

CHARLTON ABBOTS

UPPER SLAUGHTER

Unmissable attractions

This is the part of the Cotswolds that has given us the dramatic (and in reality, rather violent) cheese rolling festival, as well as villages with names like Upper and Lower Slaughter. These aside, this is a tranquil part of the region with classic Cotswold-stone villages to visit, such as Broadway and Chipping Campden, which are perfect for a wander. Snowshill Manor, a must for even the most museum-averse, has an eccentric and eclectic collection of thousands of treasures, gathered together by Charles Paget Wade, as well as an Arts and Crafts-style garden. Near Winchcombe is stunning Sudeley Castle set in beautiful award-winning gardens.

1

1 Sudeley Castle
The home of Catherine Parr, widow of Henry VIII, Sudeley was destroyed by Parliamentarians during the Civil War. It was fully restored in the 19th century and its rooms and gardens make for a delightful visit.

2 Chipping Campden
A shop housed in a mellow old building on Chipping Campden's lovely main street.

3 Snowshill Manor Gardens
The gardens here are designed as individual 'rooms' – each one is self-contained. The newer planting has been designed to encourage wildlife.

BLOCKLEY MAP REF SP1634

This handsome village, situated along the fast-flowing Blockley Brook, is less well known than many of its neighbours but has a subtle appeal undoubtedly worthy of attention. Blockley was a silk town and by 1880, just before the failure of the industry in the area, the six mills here employed some 600 people. Many of the weavers' cottages remain, the older ones towards the village centre, the 19th-century silk workers' cottages terraced along the northern edge. One of the old mills can be seen beyond a pool near the church, while the village, with its pretty mill stream, is dotted with houses of varying ages and appeal. A beautiful garden, Mill Dene, has been created around another of the old mills.

The church of St Peter and St Paul, with its Norman chancel, is unusually large, testament to its early status. Within is a Jacobean pulpit and some interesting brasses. There are plenty of good walks to be taken around Blockley, which is blessed with a pub, The Great Western Arms, a hotel and a community shop.

■ Visit

BIRDLAND

Birdland was established by the late Len Hill, who purchased two small islands in the South Atlantic. These islands, part of the Falkland Islands group, are inhabited by penguins and a considerable variety of other birds, some of which can be seen at Birdland, along with macaws, parrots and cockatoos, in varied habitats on the banks of the River Windrush at Bourton-on-the-Water. You can watch the penguins zipping through the water via the glass-sided pool.

BOURTON-ON-THE-WATER

MAP REF SP1620

The busiest honeypot in the area is this attractive village, watered by the River Windrush, which flows proudly along the main street beneath a succession of five graceful footbridges, earning for Bourton the title 'the Venice of the Cotswolds'. A tourist mecca, and to be avoided if rural calm is what you yearn for, the village does have a lot to offer in the way of attractions – Birdland is a sanctuary for birds, with a remarkable collection of penguins in stream-side gardens. There is also a Model Village (Bourton in miniature), a perfume factory, a motor museum, the Dragonfly Maze, and a model railway exhibition, all within walking distance of each other and of the main street. Just off the main street is Bourton's church, St Lawrence's, a mixture of elements, with a medieval chancel, Victorian nave and distinctive domed Georgian tower, complete with skull on the exterior, a salutary reminder of our mortality.

Bourton can be best appreciated in the evenings after the crowds have dispersed, when a walk around its back streets and along the river is a very pleasant experience.

To the east of Bourton are a series of gravel pits which, now filled with water, have become sanctuaries for waterfowl and make a very pleasant walk by following the path across Station Road from the car park.

Just west of Bourton is a group of interesting villages, Notgrove, Cold Aston, Turkdean and Hazleton, that are well worth a visit.

BREDON HILL MAP REF SO9640

The landscape north of Tewkesbury, just within the borders of Worcestershire, is dominated by the bulk of Bredon Hill, 997 feet (304m) high, a huge Cotswold outlier (outcrop of rocks) shaped like an upturned saucer. The countryside of the area is, however, substantially different from the Cotswolds proper – building in stone is much less in evidence, and the landscape more in tune with the surrounding Vale of Evesham. The hill itself is an excellent place for rambling and indeed for brambling, because in the autumn the lanes and tracks that criss-cross Bredon's slopes are thick with blackberries.

At its summit is Parson's Folly, an 18th-century tower standing amid the remains of an Iron Age hill-fort where a number of bodies were discovered where they had fallen during some ancient battle, probably against the invading Belgae, some 2,000 years ago.

Below and round about are several villages of interest. At Beckford silk continues to be printed by hand, while at Kemerton the footpath takes you through the exotic gardens of the old priory. Overbury, with its variety of half-timbered and stone houses, is often thought of as one of the loveliest villages in Worcestershire. Bredon itself was immortalised in John Moore's affectionate story of mid-20th century rural life, *Brensham Village*, and in A E Houseman's poem, *A Shropshire Lad*. The village is noted for its magnificent 14th-century threshing barn with its aisled interior, which is now in the care of the National Trust.

BROADWAY MAP REF SP0937

Broadway is almost synonymous with the Cotswolds and yet, with its wide main street ploughing busily up the lower slopes of the escarpment, it is hardly a typical Cotswold village. Most of the houses that line the street in glorious array date from the 16th, 17th and 18th centuries. Some were inns, for Broadway was an important staging post on the London and Worcester route, following the construction of the road up Fish Hill in the early 18th century. The Lygon Arms, now one of the most famous hotels in the country, is a reminder of that period. Later, the village was the object of the attentions of William Morris, and other luminaries from the arts, including Henry James.

Most of the village can be discovered on foot. In Russell Square you'll find a museum devoted to the 20th-century furniture designer, Gordon Russell. Broadway's original church, St Eadburgha's, out on the Snowshill Road, is worth a visit. The town is overlooked by Broadway Tower, an impressive Gothic folly on one of the highest points of the Cotswolds. It is a steep walk from the village, set on the edge of the escarpment in a country park. There are exhibitions, and a telescope in the observation room gives wonderful views.

The nearby village of Buckland, within walking distance of Broadway, is a pretty village with a fine 15th-century parsonage, said to be England's oldest. The church contains some Jacobean seating, some 15th-century glass and a panel said to have come from Hailes Abbey, near Winchcombe.

A Tour of the Northern Cotswolds

For many people the Cotswolds epitomise a vision of rural England. Here, pretty golden-stone villages huddle in tranquil wooded valleys, bisected by streams, woodland and surrounded by evergreen farmland. Starting from Chipping Campden, the finest of the Cotswold wool towns, with its magnificent church and pretty houses, this superb circular drive takes in many of the highlights of the northern Cotswolds as well as several worthy, though less visited, places in the area.

Route Directions

It's worth lingering for a while in Chipping Campden. For many, this town represents Cotswold charm at its best and it is possibly the one of the most attractive towns in the area. It was once famous throughout Europe as the centre of the English wool trade. A leisurely stroll along its curving High Street of handsome stone houses should be an essential part of your visit. The church, too, is particularly fine and it is also worthwhile searching out the Ernest Wilson Memorial Garden, on the High Street.

1 From the Market Hall on Chipping Campden's High Street head for Mickleton on the B4081, turn right just after the end of the speed restrictions. Soon turn right again for Hidcote Boyce. Continue to a crossroads and turn left to Hidcote Bartrim, Mickleton and Hidcote Gardens. Keep following the signs for Hidcote Gardens and Kiftsgate Court Gardens.

Both Hidcote Gardens and Kiftsgate Court Gardens are open to the public. Hidcote, transformed by horticulturist Major Lawrence Johnston, who acquired the property in the early 20th century, comprises a series of small gardens separated by walls and hedges, while Kiftsgate is renowned for its collection of old-fashioned scented roses.

2 Drive past Kiftsgate, signed for Quinton and Stratford, until you reach a T-junction. Turn right and continue on to Ilmington.
This rather scattered village has a charming manor house and a church containing work by Robert Thompson, the early 20th-century furniture maker from Kilburn in North Yorkshire, whose signature was a wooden mouse.

3 Just after entering Ilmington turn right signed 'Chipping Campden', then left for Shipston, keeping left at the war memorial. Pass the

Red Lion pub, continuing in the direction of Stratford. At the end of the village turn right and drive to Armscote, where you pass the Fox and Goose, and turn right for Blackwell and Tredington. Soon, just after a thatched barn and a pond, turn left for Tredington. Continue to reach the A429 and turn left signed 'Stratford, Warwick'. At a roundabout take the third exit to join the A3400, signed 'Tredington, Oxford'.
In the porch floor of St John the Baptist Church in the village of Tredington are the fossilised remains of a prehistoric marine reptile similar to an ichthyosaurus.

4 After about a mile (1.6km) beyond Tredington turn left for Honington, through some pineapple-topped gates. Drive through Honington and then turn right at a junction for Barcheston. After a further 0.5 mile (0.8km) go left at a T-junction opposite farm buildings for St Dennis and

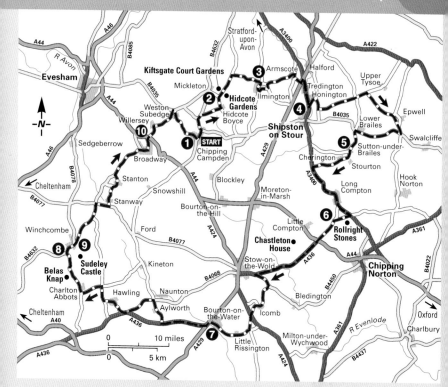

Tysoe. Pass a crossroads for St Dennis Farm and continue for about a mile (1.6km) to reach another crossroads; go forward, signed 'Tysoe', and continue, to join another road at a corner. Turn right here and then fairly soon go left towards Compton Wynyates house, and Epwell. Follow the Epwell signs. Turn right at a crossroads, and continue in the direction of Banbury and Sibfords. Continue to the B4035 and turn right, soon arriving at Lower Brailes. Drive past the George Hotel

and turn left, just after a school sign, into Sutton Lane for Stourton, Cherington and Long Compton.
Sutton-under-Brailes has a green overlooked by cottages and houses.

5 Halfway through Sutton-under-Brailes turn left for Stourton, Cherington and Long Compton. Drive through Stourton, then Cherington and continue to follow signs for Long Compton until meeting the A3400. Turn left and drive through Long Compton.

Ignore the first sign for Little Rollright almost at the end of the village, but take the second, after about a mile (1.6km) on the right, for Little Rollright, to see the famous Rollright Stones.
These prehistoric standing stones are open to the public but parking is limited.

6 There are some superb views along this road. Continue to the A44, turn right and then immediately left on to the A436, passing Chastleton House. Continue

following signs for Stow then, after 4 miles (6.4km), turn left along the B4450 signed 'Bledington'. Keep going to cross a bridge and then immediately turn right for Icomb. Turn right at Icomb war memorial and then left at a T-junction towards Little Rissington. Cross the A424 and continue for almost a mile (1.6km) to turn right at the crossroads. Drive through Little Rissington and then Bourton-on-the-Water.
This popular, picturesque village is definitely worth a wander for its pretty streets and tea shops.

7 Head for the A429, where you turn left. Soon fork right on to the A436 and after about 2 miles (3.2km), turn right for Aylworth. Continue through Aylworth to a crossroads, turning left on the B4068 towards Cheltenham. Join the A436 and then soon turn right following signs to Hawling and Winchcombe. Continue to Hawling and, some way past the church, turn right at a T-junction for Roel and Winchcombe. On reaching the crossroads at Roel turn left for Charlton Abbots. Continue for about 1.5 miles (2.4km) with some fine views along the way. Bypass Charlton Abbots and then at the next T-junction turn right for

Winchcombe. Keep going towards Winchcombe, passing the neolithic barrow Belas Knap, and Sudeley Castle down on the right.
There are good views from Belas Knap, one of the best preserved Neolithic barrows in the country. Sudeley Castle and its gardens are open to the public.

8 Eventually you come to the B4632 – turn right to go through Winchcombe.
In Winchcombe look for the 40 or more gargoyles that embellish the façade of the parish church.

9 Continue for 3 miles (4.8km) to a roundabout and take the third exit onto the B4077, following signs for Stow. Continue for about a mile (1.6km), then turn left at the war memorial for Stanton. Pass Stanway, then after about 1.5 miles (2.4km) turn right. Drive through Stanton, following signs to Broadway, to eventually rejoin the B4632. Turn right here following the B4632 Stratford signs. Turn right, and then left through Broadway, following signs for the Village Centre.
Broadway's wide main street is lined with horse chestnut trees and an attractive mixture of period houses and stone cottages.

10 In Broadway continue to reach the roundabout on the A44. Take the second exit off the roundabout, still following the B4632 'Stratford' signs to Willersey. Drive through Willersey to a roundabout. Turn right here and continue towards Weston-sub-Edge. Go through Weston-sub-Edge and then turn right by the Seagrove Arms for Dover's Hill. Continue up Dover's Hill, with fine views, to a major crossroads, then go forward and down the hill to return to Chipping Campden and the start of the tour.

Around Cutsdean and Ford

A lovely walk through open countryside that was once the focus of England's most valued export, wool. Watch out for horses being exercised on 'the gallops' along the way. Cutsdean today is a small, pretty village on the high wolds above the beginnings of the River Windrush. The origin of the village's name is uncertain: it might derive from 'cot', a sheep fold, and 'wolds', the hills where the sheep grazed; or the village might have been the seat of Cot, an Anglo-Saxon chief, in the 'wolds'.

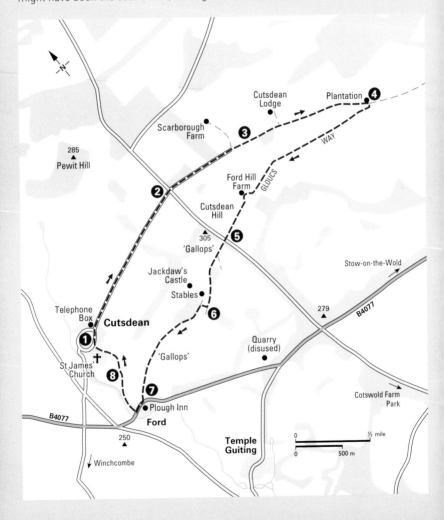

Route Directions

1 With the Church of St James to your right-hand side and, after a few paces, a telephone box away in a lane to your left, walk out of Cutsdean past Stoneley. Continue uphill on this straight country road for just over a mile (1.6km), to a T-junction with another road.

2 Cross this to enter another lane past a 'No Through Road' sign, at the margin of woodland. Beyond a second wood, where the track veers left towards a house, go straight on along a stony track.

3 Eventually you come to a gate. Through this continue along the track, initially a wood to your right, to another gate, ignoring a footpath to the left at the brow of the hill. Through the gate the path has a stone wall on the left for a field and a half, the path then goes quarter right over the brow of a slope to head for a plantation.

4 Emerging beyond the plantation turn immediately right at a track junction and right again, the plantation now on your right. Follow this track for 1.5 miles (2.4km), passing through Ford Hill Farm, all the way to a road.

5 Across the road go through a gate, signed 'Jackdaw's Castle' and follow a tarmac lane which runs to the left of a 'gallops' used for training racehorses. Keep straight on where the track veers left into a neighbouring field.

6 Soon after passing the stables of Jackdaw's Castle across to your right, turn sharp right at a footpath sign across the gallops area (watch out for horses) to join a tarmac track. Turn left. The track descends gently for just under a mile (1.6km), the gallops and greensward to your left. Continue until near the bottom, at the beginning of a village. This is Ford: if you walk into the village you will see the welcoming Plough Inn directly in front of you.

7 Otherwise turn right and, at a bend, turn right again to cross a car parking area to a stile. Over this walk along a grassy path, a post and rail fence to your right, a stream in a steep valley to your left, soon passing through a gate. The path leaves the fence and then descends through the copse to a stile.

8 Cross the stile into a field, then go half right across it. Go down a bank, across a

Route facts

DISTANCE/TIME 6 miles (9.7 km) 2h30

MAP OS Explorer OL45 The Cotswolds

START Cutsdean village or beside lane to the east; grid ref: SP 088302 (Cutsdean village centre)

TRACKS Tracks, fields and lane, 5 stiles

GETTING TO THE START Cutsdean is 4 miles (6.4km) west of Winchcombe. The nearest classified road, the B4077, passes through Ford, just to the south. Parking in the hamlet is very limited, but a wide verge beside the lane to the east along which the walk begins offers other possibilities. Ensure you do not impede traffic flow or block field accesses.

THE PUB The Plough Inn, Ford. Tel: 01386 584215; www.theploughinnatford. co.uk

rivulet (possibly dried up in summertime) and up the opposite bank to a stile. Cross into a field and turn left along the side of the field towards Cutsdean. Pass to the right of the church, which sits back to your left. At the edge of the village come to a stile: cross this to join a track. After 25 paces emerge on to the main street through the village and your starting point

CHIPPING CAMPDEN

MAP REF SP1539

The loveliest village in the Cotswolds is a gilded masterpiece. The main street curves in a shallow arc lined with houses each grafted to the next but each with its own distinctive embellishments.

As the name suggests (Chipping means market), Chipping Campden was a market town, one of the most important of the medieval wool towns in the Cotswolds. Chipping Campden then dozed for centuries until C R Ashbee moved his Guild of Handicraft here from London in 1902. The Court Barn Museum displays some of his work and that of other craftsmen.

Campden's church, at the north end of the town, is perhaps the finest wool church in the Cotswolds, with a magnificent tower and a spacious, almost austere interior that contains the largest brass, to William Grevel, in the county. The Gainsborough Chapel houses the fine 17th-century marble tomb of Sir Baptist Hicks and his wife, who built the nearby stone almshouses in 1612, as well as Campden House, which was razed during the Civil War.

Grevel House is on the High Street, opposite Church Street. It once belonged to William Grevel, a wool merchant largely responsible for the church in its current form and who, it is supposed, was the original model for the merchant in Chaucer's *Canterbury Tales*.

Just off Leysbourne, which is the northern extension of the High Street, is the Ernest Wilson Memorial Garden, a charming little botanical enclave snug in the shadow of the church. The garden commemorates the eccentric plant collector who was born here in 1876. In the middle of the village, on stone pillars, is the 1627 Market Hall.

The village is overlooked by Dover's Hill, scene of the annual Olimpick Games.

THE GUITINGS

MAP REF SP0928/SP0924

The valley running east of Winchcombe, following the meandering course of the River Windrush towards Bourton, is sprinkled with some charming villages. There are two Guitings, for example – the intriguingly named Temple Guiting and Guiting Power. Temple Guiting takes its name from the Knights Templar who owned the manor from the 12th century, and is a pretty village among trees at the edge of the stream. The church has fragmentary remains of the Norman construction, the tower, pulpit and windows are 18th century, with 16th-century stained glass. East of Temple Guiting is the Cotswold Farm Park.

Guiting Power, a couple of miles to the south of Temple Guiting, is clustered around a small green, and is a perfect example of an English village.

The church to the south of the village, also once owned by the Knights Templar, has an exceptionally fine Norman south doorway, although the interior is rather uninspiring. The foundations of a Saxon chapel have been discovered just to the north of the existing church.

Guiting Power hosts a small but significant annual music and arts festival in July.

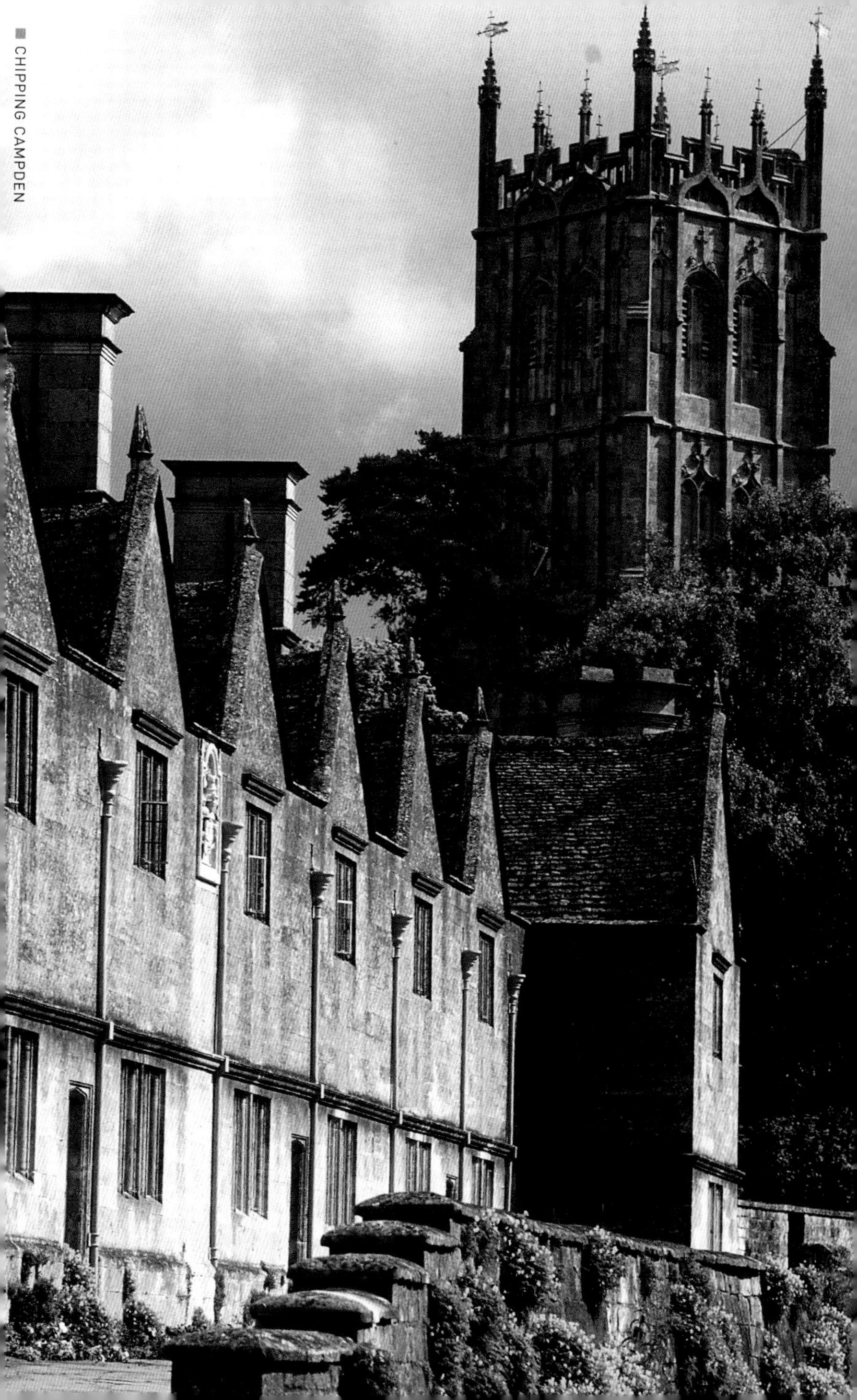

HIDCOTE MANOR & KIFTSGATE COURT

MAP REF SP1742

Four miles (6.4km) northeast of Chipping Campden, in the hamlet of Hidcote Bartrim, is the National Trust property of Hidcote Manor, famous above all for its series of scenic gardens that have transformed a 17th-century property of comparative mediocrity into an inspiration for modern gardeners.

The 11-acre (4.5ha) garden, a mix of formal design and seeming haphazard planting, was created over the course of 40 years after Hidcote was purchased in 1907 by Major Lawrence Johnston, the great horticulturist. There are, in fact, a number of separate gardens, each created to a different design, and each producing different colours of flowers and shrubs, the effect heightened by the use of walls and hedges of copper and green beech, box, holly, hornbeam and yew, which also protect the plants, many of which are rare or unique, from the severe Cotswold winds. Within the hedges are the formal Bathing Pool Garden, the Fuchsia Garden, the White Garden and the Kitchen Garden as well as a less formal creation by a stream. In addition there are a beech avenue and a lime alley. Visitors can enjoy magnificent views of hill and vale from various points throughout the gardens.

Kiftsgate Court Gardens, near Hidcote Manor, are on a wooded slope from where there are views across the Oxfordshire wolds. Although less celebrated than Hidcote, the gardens deserve a visit. The house is largely Victorian, while the gardens were created after the First World War by Heather Muir. The terraced areas above the scarp are a paradise of colourful flower beds and shrubs, while the slope is covered in pines. Above all the gardens are famous for a collection of old-fashioned roses, including Rosa filipes 'Kiftsgate', believed to be the largest rose in the United Kingdom at almost 60 feet (18.3m) high.

HILLS & COMMONS

The northern part of the Cotswold escarpment offers superb views across the Severn Vale to Wales. Best known is Cleeve Hill, whose summit, Cleeve Cloud is, at 1,083 feet (333m), the highest point of the Cotswolds hills and the highest, furthermore, in lowland England. This lonely windswept plateau straddles the way between Cheltenham and Winchcombe, distinctive for the radio towers that are starkly visible across the area. Part of it is a municipal golf course, but most of it is ancient common, bright with gorse bushes on a carpet of coarse grass, as well as birds, orchids and butterflies. It is a pleasant walk across the hill to Winchcombe, via Belas Knap or Postlip.

Leckhampton Hill overlooks Cheltenham. Like many of the hills the length of the Cotswold escarpment, there was an Iron Age hill-fort and long barrow here, built by the Celtic La Tene people who arrived from the continent from about 300 BC. More recently, Leckhampton's quarries provided much of the stone for Regency Cheltenham. The tramways from the limestone quarries went directly to Gloucester

Docks. Just below the lip on the west side of the hill is a local landmark, the Devil's Chimney, a pinnacle of stone left behind by 18th-century quarriers, and said to arise from Hell.

Just south of Leckhampton is Crickley Hill. In part a country park, it is a good place for family walking, with a number of trails of varying lengths. Here, too, are the earthwork remains of a fort used both in the Neolithic and Iron Ages. Cooper's Hill, southeast of Gloucester, is an almost sheer slope amid beautiful woodland.

On the slopes near Brockworth is Witcombe. In the vicinity, near woodland, are the remains of a Roman villa.

MORETON-IN-MARSH
MAP REF SP2032

A bustling market town strung along the Fosse Way in the Evenlode valley, Moreton is very much a roadside town, although its importance also depends on the fact that it has, uniquely in the area, a railway station; the railway arrived in 1843 and lines now extend to London.

Moreton is a place for wandering, particularly on a Tuesday when the market swings into action near the Redesdale Market Hall built in 1887 in Tudor style. The 16th-century Curfew Tower on the corner of Oxford Street was used as recently as 1860 and has a bell dated 1633. Beneath is the town lock-up and a board listing the market tolls of 1905. Just outside the town, on the Broadway Road, is the Wellington Aviation Museum.

Near Moreton are some villages worth visiting. Bourton-on-the-Hill climbs the road to Broadway and has a nice pub and a handsome church. Bourton House Gardens are open to visitors and its 16th-century tithe barn provides refreshment.

Bourton's near neighbour is Sezincote. The extraordinary early 19th-century house built in Indian style by Samuel Pepys Cockerell for his brother Charles, together with its Mogul-influenced gardens is worth, at the very least, a stroll by. Charles Cockerel is buried in the attractive church at Longborough, the neighbouring village.

Batsford, northwest of Moreton is an estate village with a Victorian church containing some excellent monuments while Batsford Park has an arboretum, and a falconry centre. To the southeast stands Chastleton House, a National Trust property, which is one of the finest

■ Insight

CHEESE ROLLING

This strange annual ritual usually takes place every Spring Bank Holiday Monday on Cooper's Hill, just outside the village of Brockworth, near Gloucester. While its origins are obscure, it is thought that its current form dates back at least to the 16th century. The brave competitors line up across the crown of what is an exceptionally steep hill (1-in-3) next to a maypole-like flagstaff. A man dressed in a white coat and top hat launches the cheeses down the slope, to be pursued hell for leather by the racers, whose task it is to retrieve one of the cheeses before it reaches the bottom. Anyone who does so, and success is rare, may keep the cheese. Despite concerns about safety, there is local determination to ensure its survival.

Blockley, Batsford and the Arboretum

This walk starts in the unspoilt village of Blockley then passes through Batsford village at the gates of Batsford Park with its 90 species of magnolia, maples, cherry trees and conifers, stunning in autumn but colourful throughout the spring and summer. The arboretum also has a falconry centre. Blockley is a pretty village that prospered in the 19th century and its fast-flowing stream, which once powered six silk mills, is now a delightful feature of the village.

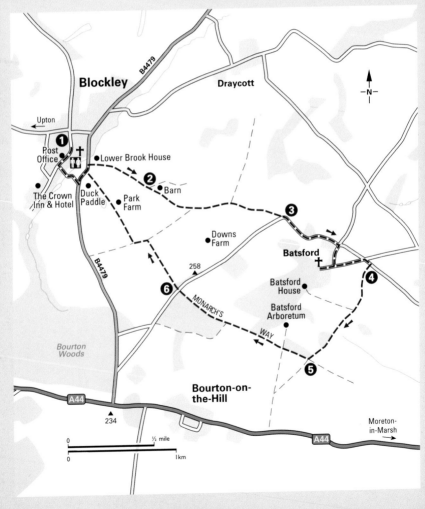

Route Directions

1 Leave the churchyard by the tower and walk through the village, turning left at School Lane. Follow this down across a stream and up to the main road. Turn left and, just before Lower Brook House, turn right on to a lane walking up for 0.25 mile (400m) until the lane bears left.

2 Continue ahead to pass to the right-hand side of a barn. In the next field follow its right-hand boundary to another gate. Pass through this to stay on the left side of the next field. Pass into another field and then after 0.3 miles (480m) go half right to a gate leading out to a road.

3 Go straight on and follow the road down to a crossroads. Turn right to pass through Batsford to a junction from where you can visit the church on the right. After visiting the church retrace your steps (there is no public access to the Arboretum from the village) to the junction and walk down the lime avenue then, at the next junction, turn right.

4 After 100 paces turn right on to a footpath and follow this through a succession of fields, negotiating stiles

and gates where they arise. Batsford House will be visible above you to the right.

5 Finally, go through a gate into a ribbed field and turn right to a gate and kissing gate just left of a gate lodge at a drive. Cross this (the entrance to Batsford Arboretum), pass through a gate and follow the path up the field to a stile. Cross and continue to a track. Follow this up until where it bears left. Turn right on to a path and almost immediately left at a wall, to continue the ascent with the park wall on your right. Keep going until you reach a stile to a road.

6 Cross the road on to a track, then go through a gate and pass through two fields until you come to a path among trees. Turn left, go through another gate, and, after 140 paces, turn right over a stile into a field with Blockley below you. Continue down to a stile at the bottom. Cross into the next field and pass beneath Park Farm on your right. Go to the right of a pond to descend to a gate and stile, then follow a lane along the Duck Paddle, until you come to a road. Turn right and return to your starting point in the village.

Route facts

DISTANCE/TIME 5 miles (8km) 2h15

MAP OS Explorer OL45 The Cotswolds

START Grid ref: SP 165348. Blockley, on the edge of the churchyard, just off the main street.

TRACKS Lanes, tracks and fields, 7 stiles

GETTING TO THE START Park on the B4479 below Blockley church.

THE PUB The Crown Inn, Blockley. Tel: 01386 700245

■ Visit

THE FOUR SHIRES STONE

This stone, just to the east of Moreton, is a striking 18th-century monolith surmounted by a sundial and a ball. It marks the original point of conjunction between Gloucestershire, Oxfordshire, Warwickshire and Worcestershire. Due to county boundary changes, however, it now stands in Warwickshire.

THE RISSINGTONS

MAP REF SP1917

The Rissingtons, of which there are three, lie southeast of Bourton-on-the-Water. Great Rissington has, around its attractive village green, a handsome 17th-century manor house and a church with some interesting memorials. Little Rissington, on the slope of the Windrush Valley, has an RAF base and a church set some way from the village itself, with an RAF cemetery. The village overlooks gravel pits, now sanctuaries for birds, close to Bourton.

Wyck Rissington, its 17th- and 18th-century cottages built around a wide green and village pond, is the loveliest of the three. From the 18th century it formed part of the Wyck Hill estate, until the 1930s when the depression forced it to be sold. In the church, which, like several near the Fosse Way is dedicated to St Laurence who was martyred in Rome in AD 257, there is some fine 14th-century stained glass and Flemish wooden plaques dating from the 16th century. Gustav Holst, the composer born in Cheltenham, was organist here in 1892 when he was aged 17.

THE SLAUGHTERS

MAP REF SP1523

These two villages with unlikely names ('slaughter' means muddy, which they are no longer) are, like Bourton-on-the-Water, synonymous with the Cotswolds. Upper Slaughter, partly clustered around the fine 17th-century manor (now a hotel) and the 12th-century church, is the more pastoral of the two. Beyond the church (which contains a monument to F E Witts, 19th-century rector and lord of the manor, who wrote *Diary of a Cotswold Parson*) the scene is absurdly picturesque – the forded River Eye bubbles in the shade of an oak tree below some wonderful stone cottages.

Lower Slaughter, about a half-mile (800m) walk away, is somewhat different in character. The River Eye is spanned by a number of flattish footbridges. The 19th-century corn mill, with its working waterwheel and steam chimney, has an interesting museum that demonstrates the workings of a Victorian flour mill. Among its collection is one of only three unused millstones left in the country. There is a gift and craft shop and riverside tea room, and free tastings of their award-winning handmade organic ice-creams in the summer.

SNOWSHILL MAP REF SP0933

Pronounced, according to some, 'Snowzzle', or even 'Snozzle', this charming and comparatively remote village is famous, above all, for Snowshill Manor, a National Trust property from the Tudor period that once belonged to the wealthy and eccentric sugar plantation owner, Charles Wade.

An ardent collector of anything that was crafted, he filled the manor house with his finds, living, meanwhile, in the Priest's House in the lovely terraced garden, without any comforts or conveniences and sleeping in an old Tudor bed. The fame of Snowshill Manor travelled far and wide, so that eminent people – John Buchan, John Betjeman, J B Priestley, and Queen Mary who apparently said that the finest thing in the house was Charles Wade – were frequent visitors.

Truly Snowshill Manor is one of the most astonishing and absorbing museums possible; of interest – with its Japanese armour, farm implements, musical instruments, clocks and toys, to name but a few – to all but the most hardened detractor of museums.

STANTON MAP REF SP0634

Stanton has a fine collection of farmhouses and cottages, most of which were built during the 17th century, the golden period of Cotswold vernacular architecture. A village of quite ridiculous perfection, it seems almost to have been preserved in aspic; and indeed is regularly used as the backdrop for period films. It owes its peculiar 'frozen-in-time' quality to the man who bought much of the village before the First World War, the architect Sir Philip Stott from Oldham in Lancashire.

Living in Stanton Court, he was determined to restore Stanton. This he did, introducing modern conveniences in the process, but ensuring by covenant that the more unsightly features of the 20th century were not to disfigure the village. A place to stroll around (making use of the car park around the corner of the Broadway road), Stanton's church, St Michael's, is delightful and well worth a visit. It has a handsomely slender spire, and a number of 12th-century features in the north arcade and also two pulpits, one 14th century, one Jacobean. It also has some 15th-century stained glass, which came from Hailes Abbey near Winchcombe. The village's fine pub, the Mount Inn, is at its far end in the shadow of Shenbarrow Hill, with its Iron Age earthworks and magnificent views.

STANWAY MAP REF SP0632

No more, really, than a hamlet, Stanway is dominated by Stanway House and its quite beautiful gatehouse. Just off the B4077 Stow road, Stanway House is reached by passing the striking *St George and Dragon*, a bronze war memorial by Alexander Fisher on a plinth by Sir Philip Stott, 'saviour' of nearby Stanton.

For a long time the 17th-century gatehouse was thought to be by Inigo Jones, a theory that has been superseded by the belief that it is the work of Timothy Strong, the mason from the Barringtons whose family worked with Sir Christopher Wren on St Paul's Cathedral. The glow of the stone is breathtaking, particularly at sunset.

The house itself, a Jacobean building with medieval origins, has changed hands only once in more than a thousand years and definitely warrants a visit. Still inhabited by the owner, Lord Niedpath, whose aristocratic presence is much in evidence, the house wears an attractive lived-in aspect; and although it contains many items of interest and value, some unique, a less fossilised atmosphere is hard to imagine.

In the grounds there is a magnificent tithe barn, which was built about 1370. The old water gardens have been superbly restored and pride of place must go to the fountain, the tallest in Britain, which rises to over 300 feet (90m). The old brewhouse has been revived and the coppers are built over log fires making this one of the few log-fired breweries in the country. Several beers are produced, the most popular is Stanney, available in many local pubs.

Next to the house is the church with a Jacobean pulpit. Near by is a thatched wooden cricket pavilion set on saddle stones, presented to the village by J M Barrie, author of *Peter Pan*. Barrie, a keen cricketer, was a frequent visitor to Stanway in the early 20th century.

STOW-ON-THE-WOLD

MAP REF SP1925

This windswept town, the highest in the Cotswolds, is at the meeting point of eight roads, and lies on the Roman Fosse Way, midway between Bourton and Moreton. At its heart is the old market square, surrounded by attractive pubs and coaching inns, shops and restaurants, for Stow's main claim to fame was as a prosperous and busy market town.

The square is not typical of the Cotswolds – its even, rectangular shape is more reminiscent of an Italian piazza, but without the arcades. Perhaps its exposed position on the wolds dictated its shape, to protect market traders from the wind. Leading into the square are a number of walled alleys or 'tures' which it is thought once served the purpose of directing the sheep towards the market place. The old stocks are still in place on the remains of the green in a corner of the square, while in the centre stands the Victorian St Edward's Hall, whose massive presence tends to overpower the more modest lines of the other buildings. Just to the south of the Hall is the medieval market cross, placed here as an appeal to the religious conscience of traders in their dealings.

Overlooking the square is the imposing Norman church of St Edward, which in 1646 played host to 1,000 Royalist prisoners following the final bloody battle of the Civil War, which was fought in the vicinity of neighbouring Donnington. The church's north door is picturesquely framed by a pair of tree trunks while just outside the churchyard, on Church Street, is Stow's 17th-century school, now a masonic hall. A fine private collection of Victorian, Edwardian and later toys, and other childhood memorabilia, can be found in Park House, the Toy and Collectors Museum in Park Street.

The Royalist pub, at the junction of Park Street and Digbeth Street, which runs southeast from the square, claims to be the oldest in the county; unlike the many other claimants for this title, remains of wooden beams have been discovered here which, tests prove, were in place a thousand years ago.

There are a number of villages in the vicinity of Stow that are worth visiting.

Activity

THE COTSWOLD WAY

The Cotswold Way is a challenging long-distance footpath of 102 miles (164km), running between Bath and Chipping Campden. It takes about nine days to complete the distance if attempted in one go, otherwise it is possible to walk short sections of the route.

Visit

COTSWOLD FARM PARK

At the Cotswold Farm Park, the home of rare breeds conservation, there are nearly 50 breeding flocks and herds of ancient breeds of British cattle, horses, pigs, sheep, goats, poultry and waterfowl. Newborn lambs and goat kids can be seen in April, spring calves in May, foals in June and cute piglets throughout the year.

A 45-minute walk (or a short drive) from Stow to the north is Broadwell, built around a large green with a ford and overlooked by a fine pub, The Fox. To the west are the Swells, Lower and Upper. In Lower Swell, beside the River Dikler, the unusual design of Spa Cottages is a reminder of a chalybeate spring which was discovered here in 1807. It was hoped that the discovery would encourage visitors to come and take the waters, according to the fashion of the time, but the project foundered. At the tiny rural hamlet of Upper Swell the road crosses a narrow 18th-century bridge near a mill, complete with a 19th-century wheel.

If you are looking to keep children entertained, the Cotswold Farm Park, to the west of Stow near Temple Guiting is a must. The creation of Cotswold farmer Joe Henson, the farm has a fascinating collection of rare British breeds. The aim of the farm park is to protect these ancient British breeds.

WINCHCOMBE MAP REF SP0228

The capital of the Saxon kingdom of Mercia, Winchcombe is a town of considerable interest, with several legacies of its past that deserve investigation. There was an important abbey here during the Middle Ages, frequented by pilgrims who came to worship at the burial place of the martyred Prince Kenelm. Dissolved in 1539, all that remains of the abbey is the wall on one side of Abbey Terrace (behind which is private property) and the abbey church, now Winchcombe parish church. The handsome church, built between 1465 and 1468, owes its present form to wealthy local woolmen. Of note here are the 40 or so gargoyles, the Winchcombe Worthies, on the exterior, said to represent unpopular monks, a sign of dissatisfaction with the abbey at the time. A stone coffin inside is said to have contained St Kenelm's body and also a piece of embroidery attributed in part to Catherine of Aragon.

Along the main street are an assortment of interesting buildings (including the fine Jacobean old school on Abbey Terrace), as well as two small museums – the Railway Museum, with a collection of memorabilia; and the Winchcombe Folk and Police Museum in the town hall, next to the Tourist Information Centre, with finds from Belas Knap Neolithic barrow.

Gloucestershire, strangely in view of its location close to Wales, has very few castles; but Sudeley Castle, Gardens and Exhibitions, entered down Vineyard Street, is superb. Little remains of the original medieval castle, but of the 15th-century reconstruction undertaken by Ralph Botelar, St Mary's Chapel, the ruined banqueting hall, the tithe barn and the Portmare Tower are extant.

During its Tudor and Elizabethan heyday, Sudeley was a place of eminence. Its owner, the ambitious Thomas Seymour, Lord High Admiral of England, eventually married Catherine Parr, the only one of Henry VIII's wives to survive him. She died here following childbirth and is buried in the chapel. Later, Queen Elizabeth I was to visit the castle on three occasions. A Royalist stronghold during the Civil War, the castle was severely damaged in 1644 and partially demolished in 1648.

In the 19th century, the estate was purchased by the Dent brothers, well known for their glove-making business. They began restoration of the castle but when it passed to their nephew, it was his wife, Emma Dent-Brocklehurst, an avid collector of anything linked to the castle, who ensured its present immaculate state. Still privately owned, the castle is surrounded by wonderful ornamental gardens, beautifully sited beneath the Cotswold escarpment; conducted tours of the castle reveal a remarkable collection of furniture and paintings, all displayed with a studied nonchalance that is a delight.

Close to Winchcombe are a number of places worth visiting. A 45-minute walk, or a short drive, takes you to Belas Knap, one of Britain's best preserved Neolithic barrows with lovely views back across Sudeley and Winchcombe. At Toddington you can ride on an old restored steam train along a scenic part of the Gloucestershire Warwickshire Railway. The railway has been reopened back to Cheltenham Racecourse. The remains of Hailes Abbey, just off the Stow road, evoke the romance of the Middle Ages, while Hailes parish church, near by, is of great interest with its medieval wall paintings and stained glass, a 15th-century rood screen and attractive woodwork.

■ Visit

SUDELEY CASTLE

Sudeley Castle, Gardens and Exhibitions has a number of delightful gardens where visitors can wander through splendid avenues of trees, shrubs, yew hedges and old-fashioned roses. Also within the grounds are a 15th-century tithe barn, a pheasantry and wildfowl area, an exhibition centre, a plant centre, a picnic area and a shop and restaurant. Special events, including a game fair, craft shows and musical evenings are held in the grounds throughout the year.

■ Insight

VINEYARDS & TOBACCO

The slopes around Winchcombe were put to a number of uses apart from nourishing sheep. The monks from the abbey made wine, while tobacco was an important crop for some decades after the Dissolution of the Monasteries until the government felt that the competition did not help the new colony of Virginia and proscribed its cultivation here.

Winchcombe and Sudeley Castle

A rewarding walk above the thriving Cotswold village of Winchcombe with its fine 'wool church', financed through income from the medieval wool trade. Sudeley Castle chapel, at the end of a long drive just outside Winchcombe is the burial place of Henry VIII's sixth queen, Catherine Parr.

Route Directions

1 From the parking area on Abbey Terrace in Winchcombe, walk towards the town centre past a Lloyds TSB bank and turn right, down Castle Street. Where it levels out, cross a river bridge and after a few paces bear right to leave the road near the Sudeley Castle Country Cottages and ascend to a kissing gate. Follow the path through the middle of a long field to a kissing gate. At a track, with the castle visitor

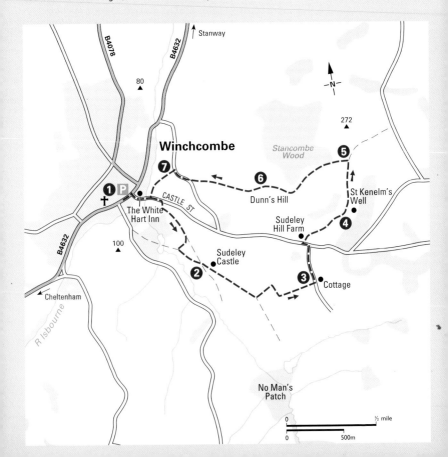

centre ahead, turn right for 50 paces, then turn left through a gate.

2 Walk between fences, a play fort on the right, to reach a kissing gate. Follow the left fence past Sudeley Castle, then across its parkland (guide posts). Over a stile in the far corner turn left and after 25 paces climb another stile and walk alongside the left-hand field boundary, then go right at the corner alongside a fence. At the willows go left over stile and walk uphill beside hedging towards a cottage.

3 Through a gate turn left on to a lane and follow this to a junction, turning left. After about 50 paces and just before Sudeley Hill Farm turn right and over a stile. Head half left uphill and over another stile. Over this cross the middle of the field, then bear to the left of a cottage to a stile.

4 Over this you see St Kenelm's Well, a 17th- to 19th-century building in a fenced enclosure. Pass to the left of this along a track. Cross a stream and go through a gate (or over the stile) and climb half right towards a gate at the right end of woodland.

5 At a woodland fence corner turn left, short of the gate, and go left alongside the fence, over two stiles alongside a small fenced field. Beyond this the path drops, fairly close to the woods on your right, and curves left to a gate. Through this continue alongside the wood, then a line of trees, to a gate and stile in the far corner.

6 Descend half right towards Winchcombe, heading to the furthest corner. Over a stile descend, a fence on your right. At the fence corner continue half right across the field. Through the hedge into the next field continue half left towards a gate. Over the nearby stile cross the field corner to another stile and a footbridge. Half left in the next field head for the gap to the right of a cottage. Through the gate turn right on to a lane, passing a buttressed kitchen garden wall on your left.

7 After about 100yds (91m) turn left through a kissing gate and head across the field towards Winchcombe church tower. Then veer left before the river valley bottom to a kissing gate by a stone cottage. Follow this path to Castle Street and turn right over the river bridge and back into the town centre.

Route facts

DISTANCE/TIME 4 miles (6.4km) 2h

MAP OS Explorer OL45 The Cotswolds

START Winchcombe: long stay car park on Back Lane; grid ref: SP 024282

TRACKS Fields and lanes, 13 stiles

GETTING TO THE START
Situated at the junction of the B4632, Winchcombe is 6 miles (9.7km) northeast of Cheltenham. Park in the long stay car and coach park in Back Lane, which you will find signed from High Street.

THE PUB The White Hart Inn, Winchcombe, Tel: 01242 602 359; www.the-white-hart-inn.com

Upper Windrush Valley and the Slaughters

Exploring the countryside around two of the Cotswolds' most famous villages, this ride encounters a succession of hills. Take your time, and you will discover scenic beauty in this pastoral countryside that is often missed when travelling by car.

Route Directions

1 Starting with the pub on your left, follow the lane out of the village, at this stage you'll find that you are pedalling easily along the bottom of the lovely Windrush valley. At a crossroads with the B4068, the honeymoon comes to an end as you take the leftmost of the two lanes opposite. Tunnelled in trees it climbs steeply away, but before too long you can start changing back up through the gears as the gradient levels past Harfordhill Farm. Your exertion here is rewarded by a fine view across the wolds as you continue onwards to a junction.

2 Go right past Manor Farm, and then left at the next turning, signed to Upper and Lower Slaughter. Free-wheeling down, you need to watch your speed, for there is a T-junction at the bottom where you should go right to Lower Slaughter. Keep with the main lane as it

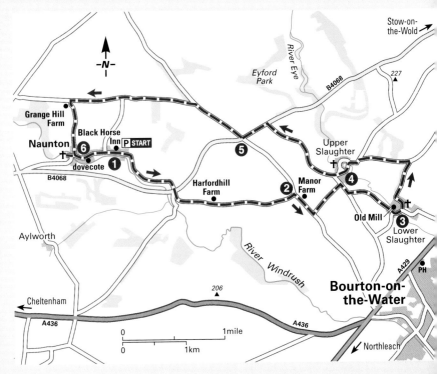

shortly bends left in front of a junction and then sweeps around beside the River Eye into the centre of the village.

3 At a junction in front of St Mary's Church, go left, passing through the more recent part of the village and the cricket green before climbing steadily away. After 0.33 mile (500m) at a bend, turn sharp left to Upper Slaughter, pedalling over a gentle rise before dropping to a junction. To the left the lane falls more steeply, winding sharply to a bridge at the bottom of the hill. Climb away on the far side to a small raised green at the heart of the village, above which to the right stands the church. Don't leave without having a look at the ford, which lies over the hill behind the church. The high ground opposite was the site of an early Norman stronghold.

4 The route continues with the main lane through the village to a junction. Go right towards Cheltenham. There follows a prolonged pull out of the valley, which eventually eases to a junction with the B4068. To the left the climb resumes for another 0.25 mile (400m) to a crossroads.

5 Turn right on a lane, signed to Cotswold Farm Park, enjoying a much easier 0.5 mile (800m). At a fork, bear left to Guiting Power and Winchcombe, the gently undulating road offering more expansive views to the south. Go past the first turning off left, signed to Naunton, continuing for a further 0.5 mile (800m) to a second turning, also on the left by Grange Hill Farm. An unmarked narrow lane, it drops steeply into the valley. Go carefully as it winds sharply to a junction at the edge of Naunton.

6 The Black Horse Inn is to the left, but first have a look at the church, which lies a short distance along to the right. As you return to the pub, another deviation is merited, this time turning right just after the Baptist church to see Naunton's historic dovecote.

Route facts

DISTANCE/TIME
9 miles (14.5km) 3h

MAP OS Explorer OL45 The Cotswolds

START The Black Horse Inn, Naunton (ask permission to park first); grid ref: SP 234119

TRACKS Country lanes

GETTING TO THE START
Naunton is just off the B4068, 4.5 miles (7.2km) west of Stow-on-the-Wold. Leaving the main road, follow a narrow lane through the village to find The Black Horse Inn, where the ride begins.

CYCLE HIRE None locally

THE PUB The Black Horse Inn, Naunton. Tel: 01451 850565; www.blackhorsenaunton. com

❶ One steep ascent plus several stiff ascents, and a long downhill stretch. Suitable for fitter, older family groups.

■ TOURIST INFORMATION CENTRES

Broadway
Unit 14, Russell Square.
Tel: 01386 852937

Chipping Campden
High Street.
Tel: 01386 841206

Moreton-in-Marsh
High Street.
Tel: 01608 650881

Stow-on-the-Wold
Go-Stow, 12 Talbot Court.
Tel: 01451 870150

Winchcombe
The Town Hall, High Street.
Tel: 01242 602925

■ PLACES OF INTEREST

Batsford Arboretum
Batsford Park,
Moreton-in-Marsh.
Tel: 01386 701441;
www.batsarb.co.uk

Birdland
Rissington Road, Bourton-on-the-Water. Tel: 01451 820480; www.birdland.co.uk

Bourton House Gardens
Bourton-on-the-Hill.
Tel: 01386 700121;
www.bourtonhouse.com

Bredon Barn
Bredon. Tel: 01451 844257;
www.nationaltrust.org.uk

Broadway Tower Country Park
Broadway. Tel: 01386 852390;
www.broadwaytower.co.uk

Chastleton House
nr Moreton-in-Marsh.

Tel: 01494 755560;
www.nationaltrust.org.uk

Cotswold Falconry Centre
Batsford Park, Moreton-in-Marsh. Tel: 01386 701043;
www.cotswold-falconry.co.uk

Cotswold Farm Park
Guiting Power.
Tel: 01451 850307; www.cotswoldfarmpark.co.uk

Cotswold Motoring Museum and Toy Collection
The Old Mill, Bourton-on-the-Water. Tel: 01451 821255;
www.cotswold-motor-museum.co.uk

Cotswold Perfumery
Bourton-on-the-Water.
Tel: 01451 820698;
www.cotswold-perfumery.co.uk

Court Barn Museum
Church Street,
Chipping Campden
Tel: 01386 841951;
www.courtbarn.org.uk

Domestic Fowl Trust
Honeybourne, nr Weston-sub-Edge. Tel: 01386 833083;
www.domesticfowltrust.co.uk

Gloucestershire Warwickshire Railway
Toddington Station,
Winchcombe.
Tel: 01242 621405;
www.gwsr.com

Gordon Russell Museum
15 Russell Square,
Broadway
Tel: 01386 854695; www.gordonrussellmuseum.org

Hailes Abbey
Winchcombe.
Tel: 01242 602398; www.english-heritage.org.uk

Hidcote Manor Garden
Mickleton. Tel: 01386 438333;
www.nationaltrust.org.uk

Kiftsgate Court
Mickleton.
Tel: 01386 438777;
www.kiftsgate.co.uk

Mill Dene Garden
Blockley. Tel: 01386 700457;
www.milldenegarden.co.uk

Model Railway Exhibition
Bourton-on-the-Water.
Tel: 01451 820686; www.bourtonmodelrailway.co.uk

Model Village
Old New Inn, Rissington Road, Bourton-on-the-Water.
Tel: 01451 820467;
www.theoldnewinn.co.uk

Old Mill Museum
Mill Lane, Lower Slaughter.
Tel: 01451 820052; www.oldmill-lowerslaughter.com

Railway Museum
Gloucester Street,
Winchcombe.
Tel: 01242 609305

Sezincote
Moreton-in-Marsh.
Tel: 01386 700444;
www.sezincote.co.uk

Snowshill Manor
Tel: 01386 852410;
www.nationaltrust.org.uk

Stanway House
Tel: 01386 584469;
www.stanwayfountain.co.uk

Sudeley Castle
Winchcombe.
Tel: 01242 602308;
www.sudeleycastle.co.uk

Wellington Aviation Museum
Broadway Road, Moreton-in-Marsh. Tel: 01608 650323;
www.wellingtonaviation.org

Winchcombe Folk & Police Museum
Town Hall, Winchcombe. Tel: 01242 609151; www.sunloch.me.uk/museum/index.html

▦ FOR CHILDREN

Cotswold Farm Park
Nr. Guiting Power.
Tel: 01451 850307
www.cotswoldfarmpark.co.uk

Dragonfly Maze
Bourton-on-the-Water.
Tel: 0845 459 7469

Giffords Circus
Tel: 01242 572573;
www.giffordscircus.com
Various locations.

Toy and Collectors Museum
Park Street, Stow-on-the-Wold. Tel: 01451 830159;
www.thetoymuseum.co.uk

▦ SHOPPING

Moreton-in-Marsh
Market in town centre, Tue.

Stow-on-the-Wold
Farmers' Market, The Square, 2nd Thu of month.

Winchcombe
Farmers' Market, town centre, 3rd Sat of month.

LOCAL SPECIALITIES

Pottery
Bredon Pottery,
Bredon. Tel:01684 773417;
www.bredonpottery.co.uk
Winchcombe Pottery,
Broadway Road,
Winchcombe.
Tel: 01242 602462; www.winchcombepottery.co.uk

Silk Printing
Beckford Silk, Ashton Road,
Beckford near Tewkesbury.
Tel: 01386 881507;
www.beckfordsilk.co.uk

Silverware
Hart Silver-Smiths, Sheep Street, Chipping Campden.
Tel: 01386 841100;
www.hartsilversmiths.co.uk

▦ OUTDOOR ACTIVITIES

ANGLING
Aston Magna Pool
Permits from Batsford Estate Office. Tel: 01608 650425

ARCHERY
Aston Magna
Rob Ireland Activity Days
Tel: 01368 701683;
www.robireland.co.uk

CLAY PIGEON SHOOTING
Coberley
Chatcombe Estate Shooting School, Chatcombe, Coberley.
Tel: 01242 870391

COUNTRY PARKS & NATURE RESERVES
Broadway Tower Country Park. Tel: 01386 852390;
www.broadwaytower.co.uk

Crickley Hill, near Leckhampton.

CYCLING
Hartwells Cotswolds Cycle Hire, High Street, Bourton-on-the-Water.
Tel: 01451 820405;
www.hartwells.supanet.com

GUIDED WALKS
Cotswolds Walking Holidays Ltd, Winchcombe Street, Cheltenham.
Tel: 01242 518888;
www.cotswoldwalks.com
The Voluntary Wardens
Tel: 01451 862008;
www.cotswoldsaonb.org.uk

HILL-CLIMB
Motor speed hill-climbs at Prescott, 2 miles (3.2km) west of Winchcombe.
Tel: 01242 673136; www.prescott-hillclimb.com

▦ ANNUAL EVENTS & CUSTOMS

Chipping Campden
Dover's Hill Olimpick Games and Scuttlebrook Wake, Spring Bank Holiday.
www.olimpickgames.co.uk

Cooper's Hill
Cheese Rolling, Spring Bank Holiday Mon.

Cranham
Annual Feast & Ox Roast, Aug.

Guiting Power
Guiting Festival, Jul.

Moreton-in-Marsh
Agricultural Show, Sep.

NORTHERN COTSWOLDS

Tea Rooms

The Mad Hatter

Victoria Street, Bourton-on-the-Water GL54 2BX
Tel: 01451 821508;
www.the-mad-hatter-tearoom.co.uk
This lovely 18th-century building beside the River Windrush is a treat. Enjoy their cream teas, home-made cakes and lovely garden.

Tisanes

21 The Green, Broadway WR12 7AA
Tel: 01386 853296;
www.tisanes-tearooms.co.uk
They serve wonderful cream teas, as well as an unusual and extensive variety of sandwiches and lunches in this pretty 17th-century stone building on the High Street.

Badgers Hall

High Street, Chipping Campden GL55 6HB
Tel: 01386 840839;
www.badgershall.co.uk
A true taste of the Cotswolds: the building is 15th-century, honey-coloured stone with exposed oak beams, mullioned windows and open fireplaces. Home-made cakes, scones and pastries are freshly baked on the premises using local produce. They also have charming rooms available.

The Marshmallow

High Street, Moreton-in-Marsh GL56 0AT
Tel: 01608 651536;
www.marshmallow-tea-restaurant.co.uk
Behind the attractive frontage covered in Virginia creeper, is a stone-flagged courtyard with tables and hanging baskets – the ideal setting for tea in the summer.

Juri's Tearoom

High Street, Winchcombe GL54 5LJ
Tel: 01242 602469;
www.juris-tearoom.co.uk
On the High Street of this lovely village, Juri's traditional stone tea room is run by a Japanese family who are dedicated to maintaining high standards. Their freshly made cakes are first class.

Pubs

Eight Bells

Church Street, Chipping Campden GL55 6JG
Tel: 01386 840371;
www.eightbellsinn.co.uk
This is the oldest inn in Chipping Campden and is near the famous church. It has two cosy bars, a smart dining room and a very pleasant terrace at the back. They serve a good range of local food at lunchtime and in the evenings.

Horse and Groom

Bourton-on-the-Hill GL56 9AQ. Tel: 01386 700417;
www.horseandgroom.info
The historic character of this beautiful Grade II Georgian inn has been retained thanks to sensitive modernisation. The top-quality food and accommodation have garnered several awards guaranteeing and enjoyable meal or overnight stay.

Plough Inn

Ford, near Temple Guiting GL54 5RU. Tel: 01386 584215;
www.theploughinnatford.co.uk
There are horseracing associations everywhere in this pub. Flagstone floors, burning fires and old furnishings create a very cosy atmosphere, where the food is prepared to a high standard from local produce. Some accommodation is available.

Horse and Groom Inn

Upper Oddington GL56 0XH
Tel: 01451 830584;
www.horseandgroom.uk.com
Aiming to serve the best pub food in the Cotswolds, this immaculate 16th-century stone pub changes the specials board twice daily. The food is imaginative, the beers are local and the setting is glorious.

Severn Vale

4 Walk start point
2 Tour start point

HEREFORDSHIRE

Ross-on-Wye

Ledbury

Bredon

Tewkesbury

Deerhurst

Apperley

Bishop's Cleve

Coombe Hill

Southam

5 Ashleworth

Norton

Cheltenham 2

Longford

Churchdown

Charlton Kings

Gloucester

Shurdington

Brockworth

Whaddon

Longney

Epney

Arlingham 4

Frampton on Severn

GLOUCESTERSHIRE

Eastington

Stroud

Slimbridge

Newtown

Berkeley

Stinchcombe

Dursley

Newport

Woodford

Rockhampton

Falfield

Thornbury

Tytherington

Iron Acton

Chipping Sodbury

Yate

Cinderford

Lydney

River Severn

Bristol

The Severn Vale lies between the Cotswold escarpment and the River Severn, Britain's longest river; along the banks of the Severn are the flat fertile lands of the Vale of Berkeley. The Severn Vale, with its brick houses and half-timbered cottages, is quite different in character from the mellow stone villages of the wolds, yet wold and vale are closely linked – they both, to a large extent, belong to Gloucestershire and many of the historical events that have shaped the county have taken place in the towns of the vale and wold – consequently, they are almost inseparable.

GLOUCESTER CATHEDRAL

TEWKESBURY

Unmissable attractions

This western area of the Cotswolds takes in two of the region's major towns, Cheltenham and Gloucester. Cheltenham is a Regency delight with elegant architecture, antique shops, the Pump Rooms, and an art gallery and museum to visit. Gloucester has as its main draw a thousand-year-old cathedral, as well as an Antiques Centre and the National Waterways Museum. For another ancient gem visit Odda's Chapel at Deerhurst, which is a complete Saxon chapel. Nature lovers should head for the Wildfowl and Wetlands Trust at Slimbridge which, impressively, has one of the greatest collections of waterfowl in the world.

1 Odda's Chapel
The chapel at Deerhurst was built in 1056 by Earl Odda in memory of his brother Aelfric, who had died at Deerhurst three years previously. A replica of the Odda Stone set into the wall tells the story of the chapel's construction.

2 Gloucester Cathedral
There is much of interest to see here, including medieval stained-glass windows. Children might be like to know that the cloisters were a location in the first two Harry Potter films.

3 Slimbridge
The Wildfowl and Wetlands Trust has the world's largest and most varied collection of wildfowl. There is also a tropical house with humming birds.

ASHLEWORTH MAP REF SO8125

This little village lies on the west bank of the Severn and deserves a mention. It is noted for its huge 15th-century tithe barn and its once fortified manor house, Ashleworth Court, both of which, along with the church, are close to the water; floods have reached as far as the church in the past.

BERKELEY MAP REF ST6899

Gloucestershire is remarkably short on castles. There are only two of note, Sudeley and Berkeley; and while Sudeley and its gardens epitomise Renaissance England, Berkeley seems to belong to the mistier, more bellicose Middle Ages. Berkeley is a fortress-like concoction of towers and dense walls, in forbidding, purple stone and was for centuries the home of one of the region's most powerful families, whose descendants have lived here for more than 800 years.

There is much to enjoy – the dungeons, the Great Hall, the Morning Room with its magnificent medieval ceiling, and a wonderful collection of works of art, including silverware, furniture and tapestries. In the western wall is the huge breach made by the Parliamentary army during the Civil War.

Close by is the Church of St Mary, in Early English style. If it is open you will find some interesting items. Among the wall decorations is a Doom painting (to urge people away from the path of sin) above the chancel arch, while the Berkeley tombs are just off the chancel.

A short distance from the castle, the Jenner Museum is dedicated to the life and work of a local man, Edward Jenner (1749–1823), who discovered the secret of vaccination against smallpox. The museum is in the handsome Georgian house where he lived. Jenner is buried in the chancel of the church.

CHELTENHAM MAP REF SO9422

Built against the base of the Cotswold escarpment, overlooked by Cleeve and Leckhampton Hills, Cheltenham is ideal for visiting not only the Cotswolds but also the Severn Vale, the Forest of Dean and the Wye Valley. It is also the scene for several festivals: a Folk Festival in February; the National Hunt Festival when the Gold Cup is run; Jazz in April; the Science Festival in June; the Summer Cricket Festival in the grounds of the Boys' College and the Music Festival in July; and the Literature Festival in October.

Cheltenham is usually associated with the Regency period, when a market town of comparative insignificance became a fashionable watering hole. The ensuing building boom has left a town of considerable elegance, of handsome,

■ Insight

SEVERN BORE

The Severn Bore, the wave that travels along the lower reaches of the river, can be up to 9-feet (just under 3m) high. It is caused by the tidal movements of the Bristol Channel and the Severn Estuary, which experiences one of the greatest tidal ranges in the world. At low tide the water recedes exposing an extensive area of mudflats, which are rapidly covered by the returning tide. The local press reports on its movements and two of the best vantage points are Stonebench and Minsterworth.

wide streets lined with Regency-style villas and terraces.

The town centre is fairly compact and can easily be explored on foot. The original town ran along the current High Street, now home to major chain stores and two shopping arcades. The Regency town spread southwards along the Promenade, one of the finest town thoroughfares in the country, today lined with elegant shops. The magnificent terrace at the northern end, built to house those coming to take the waters, now houses the Municipal Offices and the Tourist Information Centre. In front is the Neptune Fountain and a statue of Edward Wilson, the Cheltenham botanist who accompanied Captain Scott on his ill-fated expedition to the South Pole.

The Promenade continues gently uphill, passing the Imperial Garden and the Town Hall on the left, and reaching the imposing, porticoed façade of the Queens Hotel, built on the site of the Imperial Well.

The road narrows between the shops here. It is worth walking along Queens Circus towards Fauconberg Road, on the right, a short way – on the right is Cheltenham Ladies' College, part of which conceals the original Royal Well; on the left is one of Cheltenham's loveliest streets, Montpellier Street, which is lined with interesting shops raised from the road behind wide pavements. A small alleyway on the left from Montpellier Street leads back towards the main road passing old Montpellier Arcade to the left. At the top of the road is the Rotunda, now a bank although originally the Montpellier Spa,

■ Visit

CHELTENHAM RACECOURSE

A visit to the racecourse is a 'must' for anyone interested in watching the world's best chasers and hurdlers. The track is best known for the National Hunt Festival in March, the top three-day meeting of the season which features the Gold Cup and Champion Hurdle and attracts more than 50,000 spectators. The Hall of Fame tells the story of the history of the racecourse.

its design was apparently based on the Pantheon in Rome. The well preserved interior is worth a look.

If you have the time there is a good deal more Regency architecture to enjoy in the area close to Montpellier, notably in Lansdowne, which is just to the west of Montpellier. Heading southeast will take you to Suffolk Square, just beyond which, along Suffolk Parade and Suffolk Road, are some independent antique and curio shops.

North of the High Street is Pittville and its showpiece, the Pittville Pump Rooms. The Pump Rooms constitute a magnificent architectural ensemble and were designed between 1825 and 1830 by a local man, John Forbes. They were to be the focal point of Joseph Pitt's Pittville Estate. His legacies are the Pump Rooms, Pittville Park with its lake surrounded by villas in an array of fantastic styles, Pittville Lawn, and Clarence Square and Wellington Square. In the Pump Rooms, which are often used for concerts and recitals, you can taste the waters or visit the museum on the upper floor.

CHELTENHAM

The town's art gallery and museum, on Clarence Street, deserves a visit. While the collection is an eclectic one, there are several areas of specialisation, notably the work of the 19th-century Arts and Crafts Movement, an impressive display of oriental porcelain, and an exhibition devoted to the life of the Antarctic explorer, Edward Wilson.

Cheltenham's most famous son is the composer Gustav Holst, who was born here in 1874. The house where he grew up in Clarence Road is now a museum dedicated, in part, to the life of the composer and partly to an evocation of life in the Regency and Victorian city.

A number of villages in the vicinity of Cheltenham are worth visiting. Many are mentioned under their own heading but, among those that are not, Prestbury, home of the racecourse, must not be overlooked as it claims to be the most haunted village in Britain. Syde and Brimpsfield, 5 miles (8km) to the south of Cheltenham, are noted for their interesting churches; and Miserden, an estate village of some charm is close to Misarden Park, a 17th-century mansion set in lovely gardens which are open to the public.

DEERHURST & ODDA'S CHAPEL MAP REF SO8730

An attractive vale farming village of cottages in a variety of styles, with some fine examples of cruck-construction timber-framed houses, Deerhurst is splendidly located on the wide, grassy east bank of the Severn. Its claims to fame are a largely Saxon parish church and an almost complete Saxon chapel.

■ Visit

DECORATIVE IRONWORK
Cheltenham is noted for its ironwork which decorates many of the early buildings of the town. Distinctive balconies of finely wrought iron adorn many of the elegant buildings, adding a continental atmosphere to the streets and squares. Particularly fine examples are to be found along Oxford Parade, Royal Parade and Suffolk Square.

St Mary's Priory, was once part of an important 8th-century monastery. The church is the only remaining Saxon monastic church in the country and has several Saxon doors and windows and a 9th-century font (said to be the finest in England). Particularly striking is the double-headed window high up on the west wall, which is possibly made up of Roman stones; the animal-headed label stops (the carved ends of dripstones) in the middle doorway below date from the early 9th century. The Deerhurst Angel is the name of a carving, also from the 9th century, on the surviving arch of the Saxon apse, now on the east exterior.

A mere 200 yards (183m) southwest of the church is a stone building seemingly tacked onto a Tudor farmhouse. This is Odda's Chapel, once concealed behind walls added throughout later centuries and only revealed as a complete Saxon chapel in 1885. The discovery of an inscribed tablet, the Odda Stone, dates its construction to 1056. When discovered the chancel had been divided with floors, while the nave had become a kitchen.

The Severn Bore at Arlingham

This is a fairly long but quite level walk along the River Severn, the river where England's regular tidal wave rushes in. The Severn Bore, as the wave is known, is formed a little way downstream, where the river narrows at Sharpness.

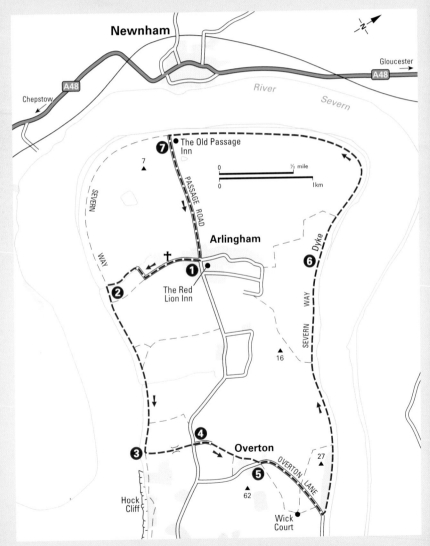

Route Directions

1 From the centre of the village, with The Red Lion Inn at your back, walk along a 'No Through Road'. Pass the church and continue along the road. It becomes a track which brings you to a kissing gate. Go to the top of the bank.

2 With the River Severn on your right, turn left through a kissing gate. Continue along this route, passing through kissing gates where they arise, until you see Hock Cliff in front of you. Pass into the field that begins to slope up towards the cliff.

3 Turn sharp left to walk down the bank and along the left side of a field. Cross a bridge into the next field. When the field edge swings right go ahead and left to a footpath sign beyond a farm track. Follow this path running between hedges.

4 Cross a road and enter the 'No Through Road' in front of you. Follow it towards some houses. Just before a gateway turn left through two kissing gates into a field. Follow its right-hand side to a stile and then continue on the same line. Just beyond two big houses on your right and about 100yds (91m)

before some farm buildings, turn right over a stile into a field. Crossing this diagonally brings you to a kissing gate and a lane.

5 Turn left and follow the lane through Overton for just over 0.5 mile (800m). Where the road goes sharply right beside a long house, turn left to rejoin the Severn Way. The path will lead away from the river briefly, among trees, to emerge at a stile beside a meadow. Continue walking ahead, maintaining your direction, passing through gates, always with the River Severn on your right and again ignoring any paths leading inland.

6 The footpath will soon take the form of a raised bank, or dyke. It reaches its northernmost point then swings to the south, just after passing a farm – the town of Newnham should now be clearly visible on the opposite bank. Continue to a pub, The Old Passage Inn, on your left.

7 Beyond the inn take the long, straight lane on your left, which leads across the flood plain, all the way back to Arlingham.

Route facts

DISTANCE/TIME
7.5 miles (12.1km) 3h30

MAP OS Explorer OL14
Wye Valley & Forest of Dean

START You will find roadside parking in the centre of the village near The Red Lion. Arlingham village; grid ref: ST 708109

TRACKS Tracks, fields and lanes, 8 stiles

GETTING TO THE START
Arlingham occupies a promontory of the River Severn, 9 miles (14.5km) southwest of Gloucester and not far from Junction 13 on the M5.

THE PUB The Red Lion, Arlingham, near the start of the route.
Tel: 01452 740700

❶ Although quite long the walk is suitable for all ages with no real hazards.

Cheltenham and Cirencester

This drive, beginning and ending in the splendidly preserved Regency town of Cheltenham – a good base for touring the Cotswolds – will take you through some delightful, but lesser-known (and less busy) areas of the Cotswolds as well as through pretty Burford and Cirencester. The route passes through some of the most beautiful villages in the Cotswolds, some of which, such as Bibury and Sheepscombe, inspired artists and authors alike.

Route Directions

Explore the heart of Cheltenham. This Regency town (it received the royal approval of George III) is renowed for its handsome terraces, wrought-iron balconies, green leafy thoroughfares, parks, floral displays, horse racing, a music festival in July and a literature festival in October. The town spreads south along The Promenade, a wide pedestrianised, leafy street with pavement cafés and elegant shops.

1 From Cheltenham take the A40 London road to pass through Charlton Kings, where author Lewis Carroll was inspired to write *Alice Through the Looking Glass*, and then pass by Dowdeswell Reservoir, built to supply drinking water to Cheltenham. Shortly afterwards, turn right to Dowdeswell, to climb fairly steeply up the Cotswold escarpment. Follow this country lane, crossing three

sets of crossroads, towards Withington. Go through the village, with its large monastery church, pass the Mill Inn and turn right signed 'Chedworth Villa and Yanworth'. Follow a still narrower country lane around the solitary manor farmhouse and gallery of Compton Cassey, until the road breaks off for the Roman villa. The remains of Chedworth Villa, excavated in 1864, considered to be the finest in the country, are set in a pretty wooded combe. There are fine 4th-century mosaics, two bathhouses, a hypocaust (underfloor heating system) and a good museum.

2 After visiting the villa, pass through Yanworth and head onwards for Northleach. Drive through the Market Place, turn right into the High Street and soon after turn left. At the next T-junction, turn right for Farmington. Go through Farmington village and then follow the lanes along the

delightfully named Windrush Valley and its quiet villages of Sherborne (Sherborne House is said to be haunted) and Windrush. Turn right towards Little Barrington.

With its picture-perfect post office and large village green, Little Barrington is situated at the heart of stone-producing country and was once the home of Thomas Strong, who was the master mason for St Paul's Cathedral.

3 Pass through Little Barrington, continue to the A40 and turn left. Bypass Burford by continuing across a roundabout and then, after a mile (1.6km), turn sharp left and then make a right turn for Widford and then Swinbrook. The pretty village of Swinbrook is associated with the five Mitford sisters, two of whom are buried in the churchyard.

4 Leave Swinbrook and take the first left after the church. Proceed along a single track road to a reach a junction

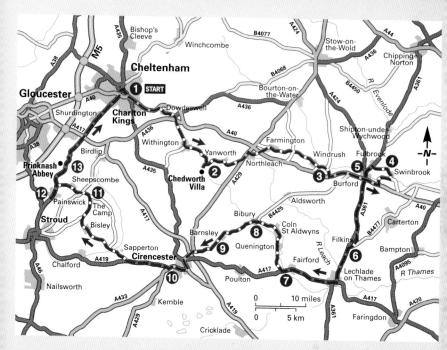

with A361, turn left and left again at a mini-roundabout to cross a medieval bridge into Burford.

One of the loveliest of Cotswold villages, Burford slopes down to the Windrush and has a plethora of shops, inns and delightful houses. The High Street runs down between lime trees and mellow stone houses to a narrow three-arched bridge over the River Windrush. Take a leisurely stroll through the town and you'll stumble across a host of historic treasures – especially in the little side streets that run off the High Street. For example the Great House in Witney Street, built around 1690, and the Tolsey Museum (1500). Just south of the town is the Cotswold Wildlife Park.

5 Drive up the main street to reach a roundabout on the A40 and go straight across on the A361 in the direction of Lechlade. Continue for 4 miles (6.4km) then bear left to Filkins. Visit the nearby village of Filkins, home to Cotswold Woollen Weavers, where there is a working mill, a museum devoted to the Cotswold wool industry and a shop, and a fine Victorian church built in the French Gothic style.

6 At the far end of the village, rejoin the A361. Lechlade is sited at the meeting point of the Thames, Coln and Leach rivers. From Lechlade bear right on the A417 to Fairford. Fairford's church contains the finest set of medieval stained glass in England.

7 Cross over the river and turn right for Quenington and on to Coln St Aldwyns. Pass the New Inn on the right and, on reaching the end of the village, go straight ahead over the staggered crossroads, signed 'Bibury', and shortly turn left following the signs. Bibury was famously described by designer William Morris as 'the most beautiful village in the Cotswolds'.

8 From Bibury, take the B4425 and continue, passing through Barnsley.
Barnsley House Gardens, which were designed by Rosemary Verey, extend to 4 acres (1.6ha) are open to the public.

9 Continue ahead to reach the town of Cirencester.
In Roman times, the town was second in importance only to London. This busy market town has a fine museum, wool church and a magnificent landscaped park. The town's most attractive street, Cecily Hill, leads into Cirencester Park, laid out geometrically in the 18th century. There is free access for walking.

10 Take the A419 towards Stroud, looking for a small road on the right in the direction of Sapperton after driving for about 3 miles (4.8km). Follow this road to the Daneway pub, near the entrance to the Thames and Severn Canal Tunnel. From here take the road, on a corner on the left, which climbs up towards Bisley. To get there fork left, then right and follow the road through Waterlane until you come to a crossroads at a main road just outside Bisley. Cross carefully and go down to the main thoroughfare of this handsome village. Turn right, then left opposite the post office. Pass the Bear Inn and, at Stancombe Lane, turn right towards The Camp and Birdlip. Immediately after The Camp take the left turn at an electricity generator, for Sheepscombe.
This idyllic village is mentioned frequently in Laurie Lee's book *Cider with Rosie*.

11 Cross the B4070 then fork right for the village, passing the village hall and pub. Keep on this narrow road until you reach the A46, where you turn left for Painswick.
Known as the 'Queen of the Cotswolds', this little Cotswold-stone town slopes down to the Painswick Brook, where several former textile mills can be seen. Some 99, 200-year-old yews clipped into arches and geometric shapes, punctuate the almost surreal-looking churchyard. On the edge of town, Painswick Rococo Garden is a careful re-creation of an exuberant design inspired by a painting by Thomas Robins in 1748.

12 From Painswick, you return along the A46 heading towards Cheltenham. Continue through several miles of beech woodland, passing by Prinknash Abbey on the left, and Cooper's Hill on the right.
Prinknash is a modern Benedictine abbey with a bird park, while Cooper's Hill is the scene of the annual Whitsun cheese-rolling event, which probably dates from the 16th century.

13 Descend to the vale, and continue, via a roundabout, through Shurdington, back to Cheltenham.

Severnside at Ashleworth and Hasfield

This is a fine walk along the banks of the River Severn, visiting a huge and beautifully preserved tithe barn. The barn, and Ashleworth Court next to it, date from the late 15th century.

Route Directions

1 From the tithe barn at the start of the walk, go along the road towards the River Severn, passing the Boat Inn on your left-hand side.

2 At Ashleworth Quay turn left over a stile to walk along the river bank. Follow it for a little over 3 miles (4.8km). In general the path is obvious, but where it sometimes appears to pass through gates, you may find they are locked and that you should instead be using a stile closer

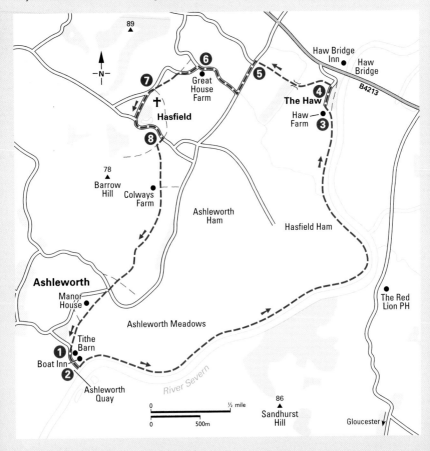

to the river. Sandhurst Hill will come and go across the river, followed by The Red Lion pub (sadly also out of reach across the river).

3 Eventually you will pass Haw Farm. Immediately after it follow a track that leads left, away from the river, and then passes to the left of a number of houses and cottages. The track becomes a lane and the Haw Bridge will appear before you.

4 Just before the lane goes left turn left over a stile into a field. Walk straight on and then, as the field opens up at a corner, bear half left to arrive at a wooden stile in a wire fence. Go half right to a stile and green metal gate crossing a drainage channel. Continue straight on across two fields.

5 This will bring you to a lane where you turn left. Within 400yds (366m) turn right along another lane, until you reach Great House Farm.

6 Stay on the lane as it bears left. Then, after passing two houses, cross left into a field. Head downhill, half right, to a corner and rejoin the lane.

7 Turn left and continue into Hasfield, keeping left for Ashleworth. Turn left to visit the church and return to carry on through the village, still heading towards Ashleworth.

8 Before a row of cottages on the right, turn right at a footpath sign. Follow a good farm track, soon crossing a stile to walk parallel with it to Colways Farm. Beyond it, begin with a hedge to your left, later drifting right to cross two footbridges, then stiles over wire fences and beside a pylon. At a lane go over a stile just left of the road opposite. Head across to a gap. Now follow the path on the right side of fields all the way back to a point just before the tithe barn.

Route facts

DISTANCE/TIME 7.25 miles (11.7km) 3h15

MAP OS Explorer 179 Gloucester, Cheltenham & Stroud

START Ashleworth Quay: Very limited parking on grass verges in the vicinity of the tithe barn; grid ref: SO 818251

TRACKS Tracks, fields, lanes and riverbank, 20 stiles

GETTING TO THE START Ashleworth is 5 miles (8km) north of Gloucester close to the western bank of the River Severn. The village is signed from the A417 at Hartpury. There is limited parking by the tithe barn (National Trust) on the lane leading to the Quay. Ensure you do not impede traffic or obstruct gateways.

THE PUB The Queen's Arms, Ashleworth. Tel: 01452 700 395

GLOUCESTER MAP REF SO8318

For a town of such immense historical importance, Gloucester has suffered aesthetically. There is, in fact, quite a lot to see, but with the obvious exception of the cathedral, it has to be sought out.

For many centuries, Gloucester was one of the most important cities in the kingdom. It was founded as Roman Glevum, at first as a garrison town on the western edge of occupied England and then as a 'colonia', populated by retired legionnaires, who were rewarded with a villa and a sinecure. Under the Saxons it regained importance in the 7th century when the monastery of St Peter was established; the modern street plan is closer to the Saxon rather than the Roman town. Once it had become the capital of a Saxon shire, Edward the Confessor held his winter court here, a tradition continued by William I, who announced in Gloucester his great undertaking, the Domesday Book. Soon after, work started on the abbey church that was to become the city's landmark, its Cathedral of St Peter. In 1216 Henry III was crowned in Gloucester (the only monarch to have been crowned outside Westminster) and in 1327 the murdered Edward II was buried here, a fact that subsequently turned Gloucester into a place of pilgrimage until the Dissolution of the Monasteries.

The points of interest are scattered throughout the city and an early visit to the tourist office in Southgate Street is a good idea. St Michael's Tower stands on the site of the 13th-century stone cross removed in 1751 'for the better conveniency of carriages', and is the meeting point of the city's four principal streets – Westgate, Eastgate, Southgate and Northgate.

■ Visit

GLOUCESTER & SHARPNESS CANAL

Originally it was hoped to build a canal from Berkeley Pill to Gloucester in order to avoid the difficult Severn route but it was only in 1827 that a shorter version from Sharpness, where the Old Dock was linked by a lock to the Severn, saw the light of day. The New Dock, still used, was built in 1874. Near by is a large stone pier, all that remains of the 1879 Severn Railway Bridge which was demolished in 1969 after being struck by a ship. The canal banks are dotted with a number of charming bridge-keepers' cottages decorated with Doric columns. If you have the energy, it is possible to walk the whole 16-mile (25.7km) length of the canal along the tow path.

Gloucester Cathedral is just to the north of St Michael's Tower, its monumental tower visible from afar. Built on the site of a Saxon abbey, it was William I who appointed Serlo, a Benedictine monk from Mont St Michel, as abbot. Serlo resuscitated the ailing abbey and began its reconstruction during the reign of William Rufus. It was consecrated in 1100 and completed in 1120, although additions were made over the following centuries. At the Dissolution of the Monasteries, the Abbey Church of St Peter was rededicated to the Holy and Invisible Trinity, becoming the cathedral church of the new diocese of Gloucester. It is an outstanding example of medieval ecclesiastical architecture, a successful blend of Norman and Perpendicular.

The tower, dating from 1450, replaces the earlier smaller tower and spire and contains Great Peter, the last medieval Bourdon bell. The nave is lined with magnificent Norman arcading, its vault dating back to 1242 together with the roof which was constructed from 110 oak trees from the Forest of Dean. The South Transept is a very early example of the Perpendicular style, while the Norman crypt reflects the original Norman church above. See, too, the massive east window of 1349 and the beautifully carved 14th-century choir stalls. Also, the Lady Chapel in late Perpendicular style, the tomb of Edward II and the Norman chapter house. The cloisters feature in two of the Harry Potter films.

The Cathedral Green is surrounded by houses from the 16th, 17th and 18th centuries, as well as the 15th-century half-timbered Parliament Room, where Richard II held Parliament in 1378.

The docks themselves have long since been redundant but the area has been restored and is worth a walk around. Warehouses have been resurrected as offices, restaurants and museums, among them the National Waterways Museum. In another warehouse is the Gloucester Antiques Centre with 100 shops to browse. At the north end of the docks the Old Custom House is home to the Soldiers of Gloucestershire Museum.

A walk through the bustle of the city's main streets is recommended. The medieval New Inn, a short way from St Michael's Tower along Northgate Street, designed to accommodate the growing number of visitors to the tomb of Edward II in the 15th century, is built around a beautiful galleried courtyard. On Southgate Street, the Church of St Mary de Crypt is a fine example of the Perpendicular style, although in its history its crypt has been a tavern and the church became an explosives factory during the Siege of Gloucester in 1643.

Some remains of the Roman Wall can be viewed under the City Museum, while Blackfriars is the finest surviving Dominican Friary in the country, and is undergoing restoration. For aficionados of museums there are several others worth seeing – Gloucester City Museum and Art Gallery on Brunswick Road contains Roman mosaics and the Birdlip Mirror, together with a Natural History section with a freshwater aquarium, and an excellent art collection. The Folk Museum is housed in half-timbered houses on Westgate Street. Not far from here is Ladybellgate House, the finest town house in Gloucester.

Just a few miles to the south of Gloucester on a Cotswold outlier, standing 651 feet (198m) high, is the Robinswood Hill Country Park, where there is a rare breeds farm. The old quarry on its west side is a Site of Special Scientific Interest because of its exposure of lower and middle lias rock, the finest inland example in the country.

SLIMBRIDGE MAP REF SO7303

The Wildfowl and Wetlands Trust at Slimbridge is the inspiration of the late Sir Peter Scott, artist and naturalist. Established as the Severn Wildfowl Trust in 1946, the saltmarshes around the Gloucester and Sharpness Canal and the River Severn have now become the home of the greatest collection of waterfowl in the world, from swans and geese to flamingos and humming birds. Excellent viewing facilities are available and, in winter, towers and hides provide remarkable views of migrating birds. There are also displays of wildlife art and many other attractions.

The village itself is certainly well worth a visit and boasts a 13th-century church, a very fine example of Early English style. Behind the church is the Rectory, which stands on the site of the early Manor House from where Maurice of Berkeley, a scion of the great Berkeley dynasty, left to fight at the Battle of Bannockburn in 1314. Slimbridge is a possible birthplace of William Tyndale, translator of the Bible into English, but so is North Nibley where there is a monument to him.

Two miles (3.2km) north of Slimbridge is Frampton-on-Severn, an extensive village which is said to have the largest village green (22 acres/9ha) in England. The restored church contains a rare lead Norman font.

TEWKESBURY MAP REF SO8932

Tewkesbury's considerable historical significance was largely governed by its location on the banks of the rivers Severn and Avon, which were instrumental in the 16th-century cloth and mustard trade and the later flour trade. Its importance depended, too, on its medieval Benedictine monastery of which only the magnificent church remains. The monastery was built by the Norman, Robert Fitzhamon, who used the Severn to import stone from Normandy for its construction. After his death the 'Honour of Tewkesbury', as the patronage came to be known, passed to an illegitimate son of Henry I and then to the de Clare family.

The abbey became one of the most powerful in the kingdom, owning large areas of sheep grazing land and building many fine tithe barns in the process – some of these survive, for example at

■ Visit

WINTER VISITORS

Slimbridge is the winter home of Bewick's swans, which migrate every year from Siberia, and whooper swans, which come mainly from Iceland. They pair for life and some pairs have been coming to Slimbridge for more than 21 years. The Trust operates an adoption scheme to help ensure their future.

Stanway. The abbey was dissolved In 1539 but Tewkesbury's citizens bought the church for the total sum of £483.

Because of its location close to two rivers which tend to flood, and with the abbey lands at its back, the town, unable to expand, folded in on itself. Throughout the 17th and 18th centuries this was achieved by building around narrow alleyways, several of which have survived (Machine Court, Fish Alley, Fryzier Alley) off the main streets – Barton Street, Church Street and High Street. Its collection of half-timbered and brick houses presents one of the finest historical ensembles in the country. The heritage centre, Out of the Hat, is an entertaining way to start a visit to the city. It is also the location of the Tourist Information Centre.

The town is dominated by the Abbey Church of St Mary and the eye filled by its great 148-foot (45m) square Norman tower. Inside, one of the most striking features is the set of 14 Norman pillars which support the 14th-century roof. The choir is illuminated by 14th-century stained-glass windows, while around it radiate six chapels containing monuments to the wealthy families that have influenced both the church and the town. The west front exterior is notable for its dramatic Norman arch.

There is a lot to enjoy in the town. A circular walk includes, in dry weather, a stroll across the Ham – an enormous meadow that separates the Mill Avon from the Severn and which invariably floods each winter – to the river.

Opposite the church is the handsome Bell Hotel. From here Mill Street leads

■ Visit

ANCIENT INNS

Tewkesbury has a number of old and interesting inns. The Royal Hop Pole in Church Street was featured in *The Pickwick Papers*, the novel by Charles Dickens; the Tudor House in the High Street was built in 1540 by the Pilgrim Fathers, Ye Olde Black Bear near the junction with Mythe Road and High Street possibly dates back to 1308, while the Ancient Grudge takes its name from the Wars of the Roses.

■ Insight

LITERARY ASSOCIATIONS

Tewkesbury has several literary associations as we have seen. There are others; Barbara Cartland (1901–2000) had links with the town and the family monument is to be found in the churchyard. The organ within the abbey church was played by the poet John Milton when it was located at Hampton Court. Daniel Defoe's observations on the town are recorded in his *Tour through the Whole Island of Great Britain*, (published 1724–26). He called Tewkesbury 'a large and very populous town situated upon the River Avon' famous 'for a great manufacture of stockings'. Seventy years later the essayist William Hazlitt, walking from Shropshire to Somerset, recorded how he spent a night in a Tewkesbury inn reading Saint Pierre's *Paul and Virginia*.

you down to Abel Fletcher's Mill (Abbey Mill), so called because it is thought to have played a role in the Victorian novel, *John Halifax, Gentleman*, much of which is set in the fictional town of Norton Bury, which was modelled on Tewkesbury. From here you can either

walk along St Mary's Road, with its attractive timbered cottages, or cross the Avon and strike out across the Severn Ham. Every year the grass of the Ham, which is owned by the town, is cut and auctioned off according to a centuries-old tradition.

At the Severn turn right to walk along by the weir and then return across the meadow this side of the flour mills. You can cross the old mill bridge and then walk along the Avon. At King John's Bridge recross the river and then turn right into the High Street to St Michael's Tower built on the site of the medieval High Cross that was razed by Puritans in 1650.

On your left, Barton Street will take you to the fascinating Tewkesbury Museum, located in a 17th-century building. The museum features a model of the Battle of Tewkesbury. Church Street, to your right, takes you past the distinctive Royal Hop Pole Hotel, which featured famously in Charles Dickens' novel *The Pickwick Papers*. Beyond this is a row of restored 15th-century cottages built by medieval merchants. One, known as the Merchant's House, is presented as it would have looked in its heyday. Another, the John Moore Countryside Museum, takes its name from the local writer whose stories were based on Tewkesbury, and the countryside and villages around nearby Bredon to the northeast.

On the right, an alleyway leads down to the Old Baptist Chapel and Court. Although the building dates back to the 15th century, it became a chapel only in the 17th century.

■ Activity

'BLOODY MEADOW'

After the Battle of Tewkesbury in 1417, perhaps the most decisive battle of the Wars of the Roses, many of the defeated Lancastrian troops sought sanctuary in the church but were slain nonetheless. 'Bloody Meadow' as the battlefield came to be known, is south of the church, off Lincoln Green Lane, and there is a 'Battlefield Trail' to follow.

THORNBURY   MAP REF ST6390

An attractive market town just north of Bristol in the county of Gloucestershire, Thornbury is well known for its Tudor castle, built in 1510 by Edward Stafford, 3rd Duke of Buckingham, Constable of England. After the Duke was executed on charges of treason, Thornbury Castle was appropriated by Henry VIII and he stayed here with Anne Boleyn in 1535. Mary Tudor returned the castle to the Staffords but after the Civil War it fell to ruin until 1824 when it became the residence of the Howard family. Now a luxury hotel, it is particularly noted for the handsome brick double chimney and the fine tracery of its oriel windows.

The Church of St Mary the Virgin has a fine medieval tower which apparently sways 6 inches (15cm) when the peal of eight bells is rung. Inside there is an unusual medieval stone pulpit. A cottage on Chapel Street houses Thornbury and District Museum, with its exhibits on local life and heritage. The museum hosts events and organises guided walks. A way-marked heritage trail starts at the town hall in the High Street.

■ TOURIST INFORMATION CENTRES

Cheltenham
Cheltenham Municipal Offices, 77 The Promenade.
Tel: 01242 522878; www.visitcheltenham.gov.uk

Gloucester
28 Southgate Street.
Tel: 01452 396572

Tewkesbury
100 Church Street.
Tel: 01684 295027;
www.tewkesburybc.gov.uk

Thornbury
The Town Hall, Old Police Station, High Street.
Tel: 01454 281638

■ PLACES OF INTEREST

Ashleworth Tithe Barn
Tel: 01452 814213;
www.nationaltrust.org.uk

Berkeley Castle
Tel: 01453 810332; www.berkeley-castle.com
Also butterfly house.

Cheltenham Art Gallery and Museum
Clarence Street, Cheltenham.
Tel: 01242 237431; www.cheltenhammuseum.org.uk

Cheltenham Racecourse Hall of Fame
The Racecourse, Prestbury Park, Cheltenham.
Tel: 01242 539538

City Museum and Art Gallery
Brunswick Road, Gloucester.
Tel: 01452 396131;
www.gloucester.gov.uk

Conderton Pottery
Conderton, near Tewkesbury.
Tel: 01386 725387;
www.toffmilway.co.uk

Gloucester Cathedral
College Green, Gloucester.
Tel: 01452 528095; www.gloucestercathedral.org.uk

Gloucester Docks
The Docks, Gloucester.
Tel: 01452 311190; www.gloucesterdocks.me.uk

Gloucester Folk Museum
Westgate Street, Gloucester.
Tel: 01452 396868; www.gloucester.gov.uk. Free.

Holst Birthplace Museum
4 Clarence Road, Pittville, Cheltenham.
Tel: 01242 524846; www.holstmuseum.org.uk

Jenner Museum
Church Lane, Berkeley.
Tel: 01453 810631; www.jennermuseum.com

John Moore Countryside Museum
41 Church Street, Tewkesbury.
Tel: 01684 297174; www.johnmooremuseum.org

Merchant's House
45 Church Street, Tewkesbury.
Tel: 01684 297174; www.johnmooremuseum.org

Misarden Park Gardens
Miserden. Tel: 01285 821303

National Waterways Museum
Llanthony Warehouse, Gloucester Docks, Gloucester.
Tel: 01452 318200;
www.nwm.org.uk

Nature in Art
Wallsworth Hall, Tewkesbury Road, Twigworth, Gloucester.
Tel: 01452 731422;
www.nature-in-art.org.uk

Odda's Chapel
Off B4213, Deerhurst.
www.english-heritage.org.uk/visits. Free

Out of the Hat
Church Street, Tewkesbury.
Tel: 01684 855040;
www.outofthehat.org.uk

Pittville Pump Room and Museum
Pittville Park, Cheltenham.
Tel: 01242 523852. Free admission to Pump Room.

Soldiers of Gloucestershire Museum
Gloucester Docks, Gloucester.
Tel: 01452 522682;
www.glosters.org.uk

Tewkesbury Abbey
Church Street, Tewkesbury.
Tel: 01684 850959; www.tewkesburyabbey.org.uk

Tewkesbury Museum
64 Barton Street, Tewkesbury.
Tel: 01684 292901; www.tewkesburymuseum.org

Wildfowl and Wetlands Trust
Slimbridge. Tel: 01453 891900;
www.wwt.org.uk/visit/slimbridge

FOR CHILDREN

St Augustine's Farm
Arlingham, Gloucester.
Tel: 01452 740277; www.
staugustinesfarm.co.uk

Rare Breeds Farm
Robinswood Hill Country
Park, Gloucester.
Tel: 01452 310633.

SHOPPING

Cheltenham
Farmers' Market, Promenade,
2nd and last Fri each month.
For antiques and crafts
shops: Suffolk Road, Suffolk
Parade.

Gloucester
Farmers' Market, Fri.
Indoor Market, Eastgate,
Mon–Sat
Hempstead Meadows Open
Retail Market, Wed, Sun.

Tewkesbury
Tewkesbury Market, Wed, Sat.

PERFORMING ARTS

Everyman Theatre
Regent Street, Cheltenham.
Tel: 01242 572573; www.
everymantheatre.org.uk

Guildhall Arts Centre
23 Eastgate Street,
Gloucester.
Tel: 01452 503050; www.
gloucester.gov.uk/guildhall

Kings Theatre
Kingsbarton Street,
Gloucester. Tel: 01452
300130; www.kingstheatre.
uk2k.com

Picturedrome Theatre
Barton Street,
Gloucester.
Tel: 01452 536168

Playhouse Theatre
47–53 Bath Road,
Cheltenham.
Tel: 01242 522852; www.
playhousecheltenham.org

Roses Theatre
Sun Street, Tewkesbury.
Tel: 01684 295074;
www.rosestheatre.org

OUTDOOR ACTIVITIES

BOAT HIRE
Tewkesbury
Telstar Cruisers.
Tel: 01684 294088

BOAT TRIPS
River Severn Cruises operate
from Upton-on-Severn.
Tel: 01684 593112; www.
severnleisurecruises.co.uk

CYCLING
Cheltenham
Compass Holidays,
Cheltenham Spa Railway
Station, Queens Road.
Tel: 01242 250642

GUIDED WALKS
Cotswolds Walking Holidays,
Winchcombe Street,
Cheltenham.
Tel: 01242 518888;
www.cotswoldwalks.com.
The Voluntary Wardens
arrange guided walks, from
easy strolls to longer treks.
Tel: 01451 862008;
www.cotswoldsaonb.org.uk

HORSE RACING
Cheltenham
Cheltenham Racecourse,
Prestbury Park, Cheltenham.
Tel: 01242 513014

HORSE-RIDING
Brookthorpe
Cotswold Trail Riding, Ongers
Farm, Upton Lane.
Tel: 01452 813344; www.
cotswoldtrailriding.co.uk

Hardwicke
Summer House Education
and Equitation Centre.
Tel: 01452 720288

SKIING
Gloucester Ski and
Snowboard Centre
Robinswood Hill Dry Ski
Slope. Tel: 01452 874842

ANNUAL EVENTS & CUSTOMS

Cheltenham
Folk Festival, Feb.
National Hunt, Cheltenham
Racecourse, Mar.
Jazz Festival, Apr/May.
Science Festival, Jun.
International Festival of
Music, Jul.
Literature Festival, Oct.

Gloucester
Gloucester Cricket Festival,
May.
Three Choirs Festival, held
either in Gloucester, Hereford
or Worcester.

Tewkesbury
Food Festival, May.
Medieval Festival, Jul.

Tea Rooms

The Wharf House
Over, Gloucester GL2 8DB
Tel: 01452 332900;
www.thewharfhouse.co.uk
Enjoy a delicious afternoon tea in this smart restaurant by the canal basin. As well as the superb setting there is a visitor centre telling the story of the area and, in particular, the Herefordshire and Gloucestershire Canal. There is also a display of works by local artists.

Thatchers Tea Rooms
101 Montpellier Street,
Cheltenham GL50 1RS
Tel: 01242 584150
An elegant Georgian building houses this welcoming tea room is an ideal place to rest after the rigours of shopping. Enjoy the calm and relaxing atmosphere while sampling a traditional English tea.

The Coffee Shop
Gloucester Cathedral,
Gloucester GL1 2LR
Tel: 01452 527701;
www.gloucestercathedral.
org.uk
Situated just off the famous cloisters, this friendly place serves teas, coffee, delicious soup, scones and irresistible cakes. Scenes in the early Harry Potter films were shot in these cloisters.

Haywards Coffee Shop
Nature in Art, Wallsworth Hall, Twigworth GL2 9PA
Tel: 01452 731422
A light and airy conservatory houses the coffee shop at the Nature in Art collection, (admission to the coffee shop is free), where a tempting range of cream teas and cakes that are all baked on the premises is available.

Pubs

The Beckford
Cheltenham Road, Beckford GL20 7AN
Tel: 01386 881532;
www.thebeckford.com
A real family welcome is found at this traditional coaching inn. Smartly refurbished it has a roaring fire in the cosy bar on colder days and delightful gardens for warmer days. The food is top quality using fresh local, and home-grown, produce.

The Malt House
Marybrook Street, Berkeley GL13 9BA
Tel: 01453 511177;
www.themalthouse.uk.com
Close to Berkeley Castle, this is a family run pub/restaurant with rooms. The dining room is large and comfortable, and a good selection of meat, fish and vegetarian dishes is always available.

The Farmers Arms
Ledbury Road, Lower Apperley GL19 4DR
Tel: 01452 780307;
www.farmersarms-lowerapperley.co.uk
This is a popular country pub with low beams and an extensive menu to suit most tastes. Fresh fish is the house speciality.

The Anchor Inn
Church Road, Oldbury-on-Severn BS35 1QA
Tel: 01454 413331
Originally a mill house, parts of this stone pub date back to 1540. Plenty of traditional English dishes are served in a friendly atmosphere, while outside a pretty stream flows by the large garden.

The Fleet Inn
Twyning, Near Tewkesbury GL20 6FL
Tel: 01684 274310;
www.fleet-inn.co.uk
With a wonderful setting on the banks of the River Avon, this popular pub offers a range of food from light snacks, to a carvery and full three-course meals. The inside has a cosy atmosphere, complete with an inglenook fireplace and there is a large patio outside. Keg bitters and draft cider are available at the bar.

Southern Cotswolds

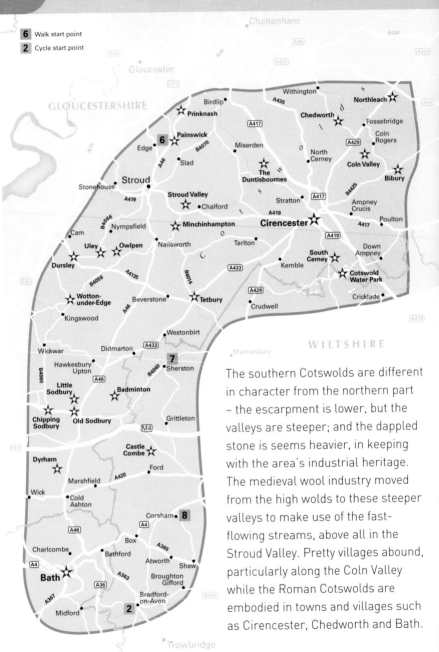

6 Walk start point

2 Cycle start point

Cheltenham

GLOUCESTERSHIRE

Gloucester

Withington

Northleach

Birdlip

Prinknash

Chedworth

Fossebridge

Painswick

6

Edge

Miserden

Coln Rogers

Slad

North Cerney

Coln Valley

Stroud

The Duntisbournes

Bibury

Stonehouse

Stroud Valley

Chalford

Stratton

Ampney Crucis

Poulton

Cam

Nympsfield

Minchinhampton

Cirencester

Uley

Owlpen

Nailsworth

Tarlton

Down Ampney

Dursley

Kemble

South Cerney

Beverstone

Tetbury

Cotswold Water Park

Wotton-under-Edge

Crudwell

Cricklade

Kingswood

Westonbirt

Wickwar

Didmarton

Malmesbury

WILTSHIRE

Hawkesbury Upton

Sherston

7

Little Sodbury

Badminton

Chipping Sodbury

Old Sodbury

Grittleton

Castle Combe

Dyrham

Ford

Marshfield

Wick

Cold Ashton

Corsham

8

Charlcombe

Box

Bathford

Atworth

Shaw

Bath

Broughton Gifford

Bradford-on-Avon

2

Midford

Trowbridge

The southern Cotswolds are different in character from the northern part – the escarpment is lower, but the valleys are steeper; and the dappled stone is seems heavier, in keeping with the area's industrial heritage. The medieval wool industry moved from the high wolds to these steeper valleys to make use of the fast-flowing streams, above all in the Stroud Valley. Pretty villages abound, particularly along the Coln Valley while the Roman Cotswolds are embodied in towns and villages such as Cirencester, Chedworth and Bath.

BATH

CASTLE COMBE

Unmissable attractions

This part of the Cotswolds is absolutely packed full of things to do. If you are looking for beautiful architecture, great shopping and a stylish place to have lunch, then head to Bath; if you want to explore England's Roman past there's Chedworth Roman Villa or the famous spa at Bath; for traditional chocolate-box charm then Arlington Row's 17th-century cottages are your photo opportunity and, more incongruously, you can have watery fun at the Cotswold Water Park. Waterskiing, windsurfing and kayaking might seem out-of-kilter in a land-locked region but you can do all of these and more (wakeboarding, birding, angling and cycling) at South Cerney. It's even got beaches.

1

1 Arlington Row, Bibury
These 17th-century cottages were built as homes for the weavers who worked for the mill in the village. The homes were effectively workshops as the weavers worked in them for piece rates. The whole family would have been involved, first spinning the wool and then weaving it.

2 Chedworth Roman Villa
Much of the mosaic work at Chedworth Roman Villa is thought to have been produced at Cirencester, where craftsmen had developed their own style, known as the Corinium school.

3 St Mary's Church, Painswick
The churchyard is notable for its yew trees. There are said to be 99 of them, but the trees have become heavily entwined making it difficult to count them.

4 Canal at Lechlade
The highest navigable stretch of the Thames attracts pleasure craft and canal boats, especially in the summer.

BATH MAP REF ST7464

One of the most magnificent towns in Europe, Bath is known chiefly for its Roman baths and for the fine elegance of its Georgian architecture, the result of its fashionable re-emergence as a spa in the 18th century. Although not strictly speaking a Cotswold town, Bath is nonetheless inseparable from the area, not least because its buildings are made of Cotswold limestone.

Archaeological evidence indicates that the first settlement here, Aquae Sulis, was Roman. Later, an important Saxon abbey was built, and then later still a Norman cathedral. The famous waters continued to be used, but it was not until the 17th century that the fashion for medicinal waters led to new building under the sponsorship of Master of Ceremonies, Richard 'Beau' Nash, architect John Wood and, later, City Surveyor, Thomas Baldwin.

The town is dramatically situated among the surrounding hills, presenting a magnificent aspect. There is a great deal to see in Bath but many of the highlights can be enjoyed on foot. Since parking can be a problem, use the park-and-ride system. Services run frequently to the city centre from Odd Down in the south, Newbridge to the west and Lansdown in the north.

The centre of Bath can be divided into four – the oldest part is the city centre around the abbey and baths; the Upper Town was built as the town expanded, while Kingsmead is the liveliest area at night. Bathwick and Widcombe are west of the Pulteney Bridge. The following walk takes in part of the first three areas; places not featured are described afterwards.

Queen Square was John Wood's first important work and takes its name from Queen Caroline, consort of George II. The obelisk in the centre was built to honour the visit of the Prince and Princess of Wales in 1738. Wood's masterpiece, the Circus, begun in 1754, is at the top of Gay Street, which runs north along the east side of Queen Square and passes the Jane Austen Centre on the right. The Circus is a design of great originality, the façade of each of the three floors is framed in a series of columns, from bottom to top, Doric, Ionic and Corinthian.

From here stroll west along Brock Street to another magnificent ensemble, the Royal Crescent, begun by John Wood's son in 1767. Number 1, open to the public, has been restored to look as it would have done some 200 years ago. A longer walk would take you further north to a number of other crescents, those of Camden, Cavendish, Lansdown and Somerset Place. Behind Lansdown Crescent is Beckford's Walk, replete with the splendid follies placed there by the eccentric millionaire William Beckford.

■ Visit

THERMAE BATH SPA

The Thermae Bath Spa provides the city with the only working traditional spa in the United Kingdom. The historic Cross Bath and the Hot (or Old Royal) Bath have undergone major work to restore the original use of these Grade 1 buildings. The Cross Bath has been officially recognised as a sacred site. There is also a restaurant and a visitor centre.

Gravel Walk, opposite Upper Church Street descends through parkland and shortly turns left, past the Georgian Garden, to Queen's Parade Place. Turn left, then left again to re-enter Gay Street and then turn right into George Street and right again into Milsom Street. Continue into Burton Street as it becomes Union Street and turn left into Northumberland Place. Pass through this little alley of shops to the High Street and cross over to the Guildhall. Designed in 1776 by Thomas Baldwin this has a sumptuous Adam-style banqueting room with elegant 18th-century crystal chandeliers.

Beyond the Guildhall is the covered market. On the far side of the market is Grand Parade and the River Avon and to the left the magnificence of Pulteney Bridge, designed by Robert Adam in 1769 and one of only a few bridges in the world lined by shops on both sides. On the other side of the bridge is a marvellous vista down Great Pulteney Street towards the Holburne Museum and steps down to the riverside walk.

Turning right along Grand Parade will bring you to Orange Grove. Pass the east end of the abbey and continue down Terrace Walk. By the Huntsman Inn, turn right down North Parade Passage to Sally Lunn's House, built in 1622 and one of the oldest houses in Bath. Here Sally Lunn created her famous Bath buns and the original faggot oven and period kitchenware are still exhibited. Although it is still a coffee house, it is also a museum and the medieval and Roman excavations are the largest on show in Bath.

■ Activity

CYCLE ROUTE

The Avon Cycleway, an 85-mile (137km) circular route around Bristol, taking in Thornbury and Clevedon, passes northwest of Bath at Saltford. An off-road route is the Bristol and Bath Railway Path, which starts from Brassmill Lane (once Green Park station) and follows the 13-mile (21km) former railway track to Bristol.

North Parade Passage emerges at Abbey Green. Turn right here for the abbey itself, the third to be built on this site. The first was built in the 8th century by Offa, King of Mercia. The 12th-century Norman abbey fell into disrepair and was replaced by this smaller version. Inside, after passing a manned desk where 'voluntary' payment is expected, there is much to admire – its magnificent ceiling and windows, and array of plaques, some of which make fascinating reading. The Heritage Vaults tell the story of the abbey and include Saxon and Norman stonework and a reconstruction of the Norman cathedral.

In the courtyard, a favourite place with buskers and other performers, the National Trust shop is in Marshall Wade's House, the oldest Palladian style building in Bath. Opposite are the Roman baths, the best-preserved Roman religious spa from the ancient world. The remains of a temple can be seen here, as well as objects discovered in the area of the baths over the centuries. Next door are the elegant Pump Rooms, a great venue for coffee, lunch or even a glass of the fairly unpleasant-tasting mineral water. Any of these things can be taken accompanied by period music played by the Pump Rooms Trio.

From Abbey Church Yard turn left into Stall Street, then right along Bath Street to Cross Bath, a delightful example of Bath's former hot mineral water sources, housed in an 18th-century building and with the Thermae Bath Spa to the left. Beyond, on the right of Cross Bath, is the entrance to St John's Hospital, a medieval foundation, still offering sheltered housing.

Take the wide pavement further to the right of Cross Bath, turning left by Chandos Buildings, and continue past the back of the Hospital to the road, Westgate Buildings. Turn right until you reach Sawclose to the right. Before continuing up there have a look at Kingsmead Square on the left, where Rosewell House is a rare example of the baroque style in this Georgian city.

Continue up Sawclose where the Theatre Royal, opened in 1805, is on the left. Next door is the former home of Beau Nash. Cross the road to enjoy a good view of the theatre and then turn right down Upper Borough Walls.

Along Upper Borough Walls are the surviving remnants of the medieval city wall opposite the Royal National Hospital for Rheumatic Diseases. After the wall turn left down a narrow lane and then left into Trim Street, where General Wolfe's former residence is marked with a memorial plaque. Turn right through Trim Bridge arch to Queen Street and left by the junction with Quiet Street into Wood Street, which will bring you back to Queen Square.

There are plenty of other things to see in Bath, including notable and unusual museum collections. In Upper Town the Assembly Rooms, on Bennett Street, were built to complement the Pump Room. This elegant building houses the Museum of Fashion, which covers the history of clothes from the 16th century to the present day. Close by, near the Circus, is the Museum of East Asian Art covering 7,000 years of history to include exhibits of jade, bamboo and lacquer. On the Paragon, in the Countess of Huntingdon's Chapel, is the Building of Bath Museum, which shows how the city was created. Not far from the Assembly Rooms, in Julian Road, is the Museum of Bath at Work, which tells the story of the city's trades and industries.

The Victoria Art Gallery is on Bridge Street. It has important paintings by British and European Masters, as well as fascinating scenes of early Bath life. There are also collections of porcelain, watches and other decorative items.

The Holburne Museum of Art, (closed for restoration until spring 2011), is home to the city's finest collections of silverware, porcelain, furniture and paintings, which are displayed along with examples of 20th-century items.

Among the interesting places in the area is Beckford's Tower, standing on the summit of Lansdown. It was built in 1825 to house part of William Beckford's art collection and now holds a museum devoted to his life. Two miles (3.2km) southeast of Bath, the American Museum at Claverton Manor, a fine 19th-century house illustrates American life from the 17th to 19th centuries.

BADMINTON MAP REF ST8082

The name most likely evokes the image of either a feathered shuttlecock and a high net or a three-day equestrian event. The first, the game of badminton, was brought from India in the 1870s and takes its name from Badminton House, the demesne of the Dukes of Beaufort; while the second is an annual event of world renown that has taken place on the estate since 1949.

Badminton House (not open), a Palladian structure built for the first Duke of Beaufort in 1682, was remodelled by William Kent in 1740. It is considered a particularly fine example of the period style and the interior is wonderfully decorated. The park was partly the work of 'Capability' Brown. Some of the formal layout is on a quite extraordinary scale; the so-called Great Avenue is several miles long and lined with trees.

The 18th-century church of Great Badminton, which is in the estate grounds close to the house, is notable for its monuments to the Beaufort family, one of which, by Grinling Gibbons, is so big that the church had to be altered to accommodate it. The box pews are exceptionally large, like old-fashioned snug bars.

■ Insight

BEAUFORTSHIRE

The area around Badminton, seat of the Dukes of Beaufort, was known locally as 'Beaufortshire', since it lies in the land of the Beaufort Hunt. There is a print of a chimney sweep at Chipping Sodbury saying 'Sorry, gentlemen, I can't vote for you 'cause I 'unts with the Duke'.

BIBURY MAP REF SP1106

Bibury, one of the most popular of the classic Cotswold villages, was famously described by the poet and artist William Morris as the 'most beautiful village in England', a rather risky thing to say, particularly in an area as blessed with handsome villages as the Cotswolds. Still, Bibury is undoubtedly in the first echelon, with the trout-filled Coln river sliding alongside the main street, its exceptionally interesting church and an array of picturesque cottages.

Bibury was originally a Saxon foundation, although most of what makes Bibury and Arlington (the neighbouring settlement) so attractive dates from around the 17th century when the village prospered as a weaving centre. The church, in a well-tended churchyard at the heart of the original village at the far end of the main street, retains some of its original Saxon work – the chancel arch jambs and the fragments of a cross shaft.

Among the many delightful cottages in the village, those in Arlington Row, a terrace of low-gabled weavers' cottages just across the river towards the church end of the village, are the most famously photogenic. They belong to the National Trust, and are still occupied. Originally they were used by workers weaving wool for Arlington Mill at the other end of the village – they used the Rack Isle in front of the cottages, now a bird sanctuary, for drying wool. The path in front of Arlington Row continues up Awkward Hill, which is lined with attractive cottages, or skirts Rack Isle, parallel to the river, to 17th-century Arlington Mill.

Next door is Bibury Trout Farm where you can catch your own fish or make purchases from the shop. Just across the road is the Swan Hotel, once a fashionable haunt for the followers of Bibury Races, which flourished during the 17th century. Now it is an elegant place to stay or to take afternoon tea.

The pretty neighbouring hamlet of Ablington is a collection of cottages, barns and manor houses and the home of the Reverend Arthur Gibbs, the 19th-century author of A Cotswold Village.

West of Bibury on the road to Cirencester, is the village of Barnsley. The Georgian mansion, Barnsley Park, just outside the village, is not open to the public although there are good walks through the grounds. In the village centre, however, is Rosemary Verey's (1918–2001) Barnsley House Garden, a lovely 18th-century garden featuring herbs, a knot garden and a vegetable garden in the style of a potager. The house is now a luxury hotel and allows visitors to enjoy the delights of the garden, for a fee. Barnsley church has unusual Norman features.

South of Barnsley are the Ampneys, villages set in flat countryside with interesting churches. Down Ampney is the birthplace of the composer Ralph Vaughan Williams, who gave the village name to one of his best known hymns. There is a small exhibition about the composer inside the church.

CASTLE COMBE MAP REF ST8477

Generally considered one of the loveliest villages in the Cotswolds, Castle Combe is very popular and can get crowded.

■ Insight

THE BISLEY PIECE

Part of Bibury churchyard is known as the Bisley Piece, the result of a curious story. It seems that at Bisley there was what was called a 'bone hole', where old bones were thrown when old graves were broken into. Some 600 years ago a priest is supposed to have fallen in and died, an incident that apparently angered the Pope himself. Consequently the pontiff forbade burials in Bisley for two years, the residents having, instead, to bury their dead at Bibury, some 15 miles (24km) away.

Parking is a problem here and visitors are asked to use the car park. The perfection of this pretty village means that it is also used by film producers.

Like many other Cotswold villages, its wealth came from sheep and wool. Most of the houses here were weavers' houses, and it was allowed to hold a fair for trading sheep and wool. The 14th-century Market Cross, with the old water pump beside it, forms the centre of the village. The nearby Butter Cross was dismantled during the 19th century. The church probably dates from the 12th century; one of the interesting items is the clock that used to chime from the tower. A favourite view of the village is from the old weavers' cottages, across the bridge. The small Village Museum, staffed by Castle Combe residents, contains many items of local interest.

Outside the village is the motor racing circuit, which hosted national championship races until the 1990s. Motor sport and other popular events are still held here.

Painswick and Washpool Valley

This is a fairly long but enjoyable walk from Painswick, known as the 'Queen of the Cotswolds'. You pass a golf course then climb Painswick Hill before descending through the Washpool Valley. Painswick's friendly Falcon Inn not only has a drying room for wet walking gear, but also a centuries-old bowling green in its grounds.

Route Directions

1 Turn right out of the car park and right along the main street. Turn left along Gloucester Street, join another road and continue uphill, then go right on to Golf Course Road. Bear left on to a track, joining the Cotswold Way, go through the car park, turn left into a lane and then, after 50 paces go left into woodland and across a fairway (look out for golf balls).

2 Keep to the left of a cemetery, then cross another fairway to a path. Continue to a road. After 50 paces turn right, leaving the track after 60 paces. Walk along the left edge of the golf course to the top, passing to the right of a trig point. Descend the other side and turn left down a path. At a track go left to a road, aiming for the gap in the trees visible from the trig point.

3 Turn right and descend to a bus stop. Here cross to a path amid trees. Beyond a gate turn left down a track to Spoonbed Farm, and descend bearing right at a track junction. Pass the farm to a gate, then take a path to a field. In a second field keep left of an ash tree to reach a stile. Through a new copse and after another stile cross a field to the right of Upper Holcombe Farm to a stile.

4 Turn left onto a lane for 0.5 mile (800m) to Holcombe Farm. Here continue straight on along a track, passing some gates at a bend on the left. Continue and at a stile go left into the next field. Cross a stile and bear right to another stile. Over this turn right into a green lane which leads to a footbridge with a stile at each end. Bear right alongside the stream and soon bear left uphill to a stile. Over this follow the left-hand field margin curving uphill to reach a stile.

5 Turn left along a track towards Edge Farm and fork right at farm buildings to a gate. Over a stone stile cross two fields to a gate arriving at a road. Bear right at a Y-junction. Opposite a house turn left over a stile, bear half right to another stile and onto a path between a hedge and fence to enter Edge.

6 Turn left, then sharp right at the post-box and go past the village hall. Before the farmhouse turn left over a stile, then another and descend along the field margin to a footbridge. Over this ascend a field to a stile in the opposite hedge, then head for a gate at a track, to the right of a farm. Go through this and through another gate opposite and then along field edge to a kissing gate on to a lane. Turn left and, after 30 paces, turn right via a gate on to a track. The track becomes a path to a stile. Cross fields on the same line, then over stile and quarter left to a field gate and then another, passing right by a house to reach a road.

7 Turn left, descend to cross the A46 and walk along Pincot Lane. At Primrose Cottage turn left over a stile and then

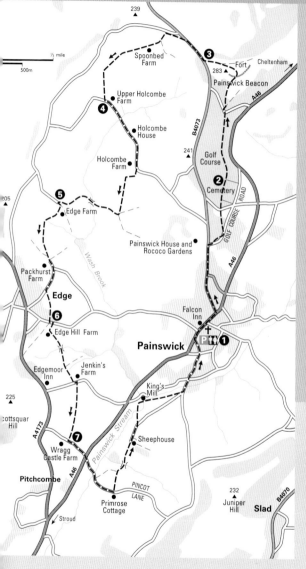

Route facts

DISTANCE/TIME
7.5 miles (12.1km) 3h30

MAP OS Explorer 179
Gloucester, Cheltenham
& Stroud

START Painswick: car park
(pay and display) near
library, just off main road;
grid ref: SO 865095

TRACKS Fields and tracks,
golf course and a green
lane, 20 stiles

GETTING TO THE START
Some 3 miles (4.8km) north
of Stroud, Painswick is on
the A46 at its junction with
the B4073 from Gloucester.
The car park is beside the
main road towards the
southern end of the village,
by the library.

THE PUB The Falcon
Inn, Painswick.
Tel: 01452 814222; www.
falconinn-cotswolds.co.uk

walk alongside the stream
to arrive at a lane, via two
more stiles. Turn left to
return to Painswick.

cross to another. Descend to
cross a footbridge, climb and
cross the field to a gate, left
of Sheephouse. Walk along

the drive and where it forks
go left down to King's Mill.
Bear right through a gate and
over the weir, then a stile, and

CHEDWORTH MAP REF SP0512

A charming village in itself, the name of Chedworth is usually associated with a Roman villa considered by many to be the finest in England. Since the two are separated by a mile or two, follow road signs to Chedworth or Chedworth Villa, depending on which you want.

Chedworth village, which is said to be the longest village in England, clusters about a lovely old pub. Opposite, a spring pours interminably and a church soars in comparison with the size of the village.

The villa, discovered in 1864, is owned by the National Trust, and is about a mile (1.6km) or a half-hour walk from the village. Although the site looks perfect for a villa, it is thought that the trees that now largely surround it were not there when it was built and that the villa was, instead, in the midst of open farmland. In its time it was one of the largest Romano-British villas in Britain. This, and other items of information are given in the short, well-produced video that is shown every 15 minutes as part of the entry price.

Most of the original superstructure of the villa has long gone. What remains are the lower parts of the walls, enough to identify the purposes of each of the rooms, and mosaics featuring, among other things, representations of the four seasons. Archaeologists are still hard at work on the site, and there is still a fair amount to be excavated in order to get the full picture. There is a comparatively recent building in the middle, which is the administrator's house with a small museum attached at its rear.

■ Visit

THE KING'S HEAD

On the Market Square in Cirencester is the King's Head, complete with royal keystone over the door. Despite outward appearances the hotel dates back to 1340. In 1642 the Royalist Lord Chandos took refuge in the hotel, thus saving his life, while in 1688 Lord Lovelace, of William of Orange's army, was captured here.

CIRENCESTER MAP REF SP0201

Now a busy market town, Cirencester was once the most important city in England after London, during the Roman occupation. Called Corinium Dubunnorum and founded as a military headquarters in AD 49, a number of important roads radiated from the city – the Fosse Way, Ermin Street and Akeman Street. The Saxons renamed Corinium 'Cirencester' (which from coryn, means the 'top part', in reference to the River Churn, the highest source of the Thames; and ceastre, which means 'fort') but practically destroyed the town, preferring instead to build smaller settlements outside the walls. Only in the Middle Ages did Cirencester regain something of its former glory when it became the most important of the Cotswold wool towns. Markets still take place each Monday and Friday.

The town is most easily explored on foot. There are a number of well-signposted car parks within easy reach of the city centre, while the market square is the most convenient place to begin discovery of the town. The 15th-century parish church of St John

Baptist, one of the largest in England, is the main feature. Its magnificent Perpendicular tower was built with the reward given by Henry IV to a group of local earls who foiled a rebellion. Its fine roof is illuminated by clerestory windows, while the east and west windows are filled with medieval stained glass. The best-known feature of the exterior is the three-storeyed south porch, overlooking the market square, which was built by the abbots in the late 15th century as an office for the abbey (now vanished) and which became the Town Hall after the Dissolution. One of the finest in the country, it was returned to the church only in the 18th century. Inside is a decorative painted wine goblet-style pulpit, several memorial brasses bearing the matrimonial histories of well-known wool merchants and some interesting church plate.

Opposite the church, is the Victorian Corn Hall, on the Market Square, which has been beautifully restored and hosts several markets throughout the week. Cricklade Street, running south from the square, is the site of the Brewery Arts Centre. This hub of visual and performing arts also has craft studios housed in the old brewery.

■ Insight

ECCLESIASTICAL TREASURES

The church plate of Cirencester's parish church is among the most interesting in the country, particularly the Boleyn Cup which was made for Anne Boleyn, second wife of Henry VIII, in 1535. The church is notable also because it has the oldest 12-bell peal in the country, which rings out the 'pancake bell' on Shrove Tuesday.

On Park Street, close to Cirencester Park, is Corinium Museum, which brings to life many aspects of local history and various finds, including the mosaics that were made in the area from the Roman and later eras. Many are displayed in tableaux form. It is also the home of the Tourist Information Centre.

Close by is Thomas Street, the location of a 15th-century Weavers Hall almshouse (also known as St Thomas's Hospital) and also Coxwell Street, lined with merchants' houses. Farther north is Spitalgate Lane, with the arcade of the nave of St John's Hospital, and another group of almshouses. East from here is the mysterious-looking Spital Gate, all that remains of the old abbey. From here a walk through the Abbey Grounds, where the remnants of the Roman walls can be seen at the eastern boundary, will take you back to the town centre.

No visit to Cirencester would be complete without a glimpse, at the very least, of Cirencester Park, probably the finest example of geometric landscaping in the country. It is approached up Cecily Hill, one of the prettiest streets in Cirencester, which leads to the wrought iron entrance gates. The park was the conception of the 1st Lord Bathurst in the early 18th century and the house (not open to the public), behind one of the largest yew hedges in the world, was built to his own design. The park was landscaped with the help of the poet Alexander Pope, among others, who has celebrated the construction of the park in verse. In fact there is a corner known as Pope's Seat near the polo ground. It is an excellent place for walking (the grounds are privately owned but open to walkers and riders), especially along the Broad Ride, which stretches from the entrance almost to Sapperton.

Apart from the wall in the Abbey Garden, the only other surviving Roman souvenir is the superb 2nd-century Roman Amphitheatre, which is one of the largest and best preserved in the country. It is found on Cotswold Avenue just south of the Ring Road.

THE COLN VALLEY

The River Coln, a tributary of the Thames, is arguably the loveliest of the many rivers that ripple through the Cotswolds. It rises on the escarpment not far from Cheltenham then gently descends the slopes, passing through a number of pretty villages en route.

Withington has an unusually large church with a fine Norman doorway and a handsome wall monument to Sir John and Lady Howe of Compton Cassey. The 17th-century mansion of Compton Cassey is now a magnificent farmhouse, lying in splendid isolation in the middle of the valley, forcing the Yanworth road to curve around it. As you approach it you may, for one possibly alarming moment, see a sculpture in a field close by. If so it will be the product of the artist's Compton Cassey Gallery, which now occupies the house.

Near here the river passes close to Chedworth Roman Villa and thence to Fossebridge, a steep point on the Roman Fosse Way where an ancient inn continues to attract passing customers. On the other side of the road the Coln furrows across the meadows of Coln

St Dennis, a small, silent village built around a modest green, with a small Norman church. Look for the mysterious inscription to Joan Burton on the interior wall of the tower, as well as the Norman corbel stones that now line the nave.

Further on is the pretty hamlet of Calcot and then almost immediately Coln Rogers with a church remarkable for its Saxon plan and Saxon window north of the chancel. At the old mill in Winson, where the road zigzags, there are charming gardens and towards the centre of the village you'll find some converted barns. The compact green is overlooked by a classical looking manor house. After Winson come Ablington and Bibury.

Finally, before going on to Fairford and Lechlade, the Coln arrives at Coln St Aldwyns, where the green is shaded by a magnificent horse chestnut tree and the New Inn is a fine pub. A pretty churchyard surrounds the church, which has memorial windows commemorating John Keble, the 19th-century reformer, and his father. It is possible to walk along the Coln from here to Bibury.

Sherston and Easton Grey

The infant Bristol Avon links attractive stone villages on this pastoral ramble on the fringes of the Cotswolds. The route, which starts in Sherston's attractive wide High Street, passes through parkland and also takes in part of the Fosse Way.

Route Directions

1 On Sherton's High Street, walk towards the village stores, pass the Rattlebone Inn and turn right into Noble Street. Pass Grove Road and take the footpath on your left up a flight of steps. Cross a cul-de-sac and follow the metalled footpath to a gate. Continue at the rear of houses to a further gate.

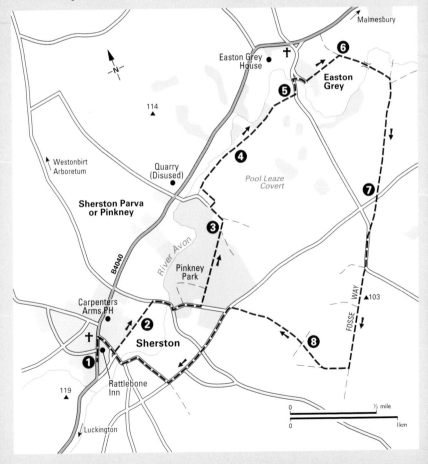

2 Bear diagonally right across a field to a stile, followed by a gate leading out to a lane. Turn right, cross the river and turn left, signed 'Foxley'. At the end of woodland on your left, take the footpath left through a gate. Follow the track across Pinkney Park to a gate.

3 Keep ahead, bearing left beside the wall to a gate. Immediately beyond it turn right for several paces, then left through a gate. Follow the path round the edge of a field to a stile. Cross it, then go immediately right over the adjacent stile. Aim for the left-hand corner of the field to the next stile. Keep alongside the fence to the next stile and bear right to a gate.

4 Go diagonally across the field with Easton Grey House visible in the distance. Cross two stiles with a footbridge in between and head downhill to a gate and lane.

5 Turn left into Easton Grey. Cross the river bridge, turn right uphill to take the footpath ahead on reaching entrance gates on your right. Cross a gravelled area, go through a gate and keep ahead to a stile. Maintain direction across the next field

and gently descend to follow a track into the next field.

6 Turn right along the field-edge and bear off right in the corner, downhill through scrub to a footbridge. Keep ahead beside a ruin to a gate. Cross a stile and continue to a further stile and gate. Follow the track downhill to a stile and turn right along a track (Fosse Way). Continue for just over 0.5 mile (around 900m) to a road.

7 Cross straight over and keep to the byway to another road. Bear left and keep ahead where the lane veers sharp left. Follow this rutted track for 0.5 mile (800m), then cross the arrowed stile on your right. Head across the field to a stile and continue ahead beside a hedge to a gate. Turn right then immediately left, skirt a paddock and join a track.

8 Cross a racehorse gallop to a gate. Walk through scrub to another gate and keep to the track ahead to a road. Turn left and continue to a crossroads. Proceed straight on to the next junction and keep ahead, following the lane all the way back into Sherston and the start of the walk.

Route facts

DISTANCE/TIME
6.5 miles (10.4km) 3h

MAP OS Explorer 168 Stroud, Tetbury & Malmesbury

START Sherston High Street; plenty of roadside parking; grid ref: ST 853858

TRACKS Field and parkland paths, tracks, metalled lanes, 13 stiles

GETTING TO THE START
Sherston stands midway between Bath and Cirencester on the B4040, 5 miles (8km) west of Malmesbury. There is parking beside the wide High Street.

THE PUB The Rattlebone Inn, Sherston. Tel: 01666 840871

■ Insight

WILLIAM TYNDALE

Southwest of Dursley is Nibley Knoll with its distinctive needle-shaped monolith rising out of the hillside. This is the Tyndale Monument, built in 1866 in honour of William Tyndale, born in nearby North Nibley, and the first man, in 1484, to translate the Bible from Latin into English. It is possible to climb its 111 feet (34m), from where there are excellent views.

THE DUNTISBOURNES

MAP REF SO9607

A string of villages along the small River Dunt just to the north of Cirencester, the Duntisbournes have a special character on account of their saddleback church towers which have something almost French about them.

Duntisbourne Abbotts was the home of Dr Matthew Baillie, the Scottish physician who attended George III during his many years of illness. Cotswold Farm was the home of the 19th-century Methodist, Elizabeth Cross, who set up a mission in Tonga and converted the Tonga royal family. Duntisbourne Leer is prettily forded by the Dunt, as is Middle Duntisbourne, barely more than a farm at the bottom of a steep valley. The church at Duntisbourne Rouse has a particularly dramatic situation at the top of a slope leading down to the Dunt and an atmospheric interior with box pews and medieval wall paintings.

DURSLEY   MAP REF ST7598

Although this busy market town just beneath the Cotswold edge has been quite severely modernised in places, its old centre remains intact and boasts some interesting items. Nestling just beneath wooded slopes, it was once an important cloth manufacturing town and the delightfully arcaded market hall, built in 1729, and the Georgian Market House (town hall) sit bang in the centre, complete with statue of Queen Anne.

The church is not blessed with a very harmonious interior but does have a fine vaulted porch in the Perpendicular style. The tower in Gothic style was only rebuilt at the beginning of the 18th century with a grant from Queen Anne after the spire collapsed in 1698. The north door of the church was blocked to prevent its use as a right of way for the collection of water from the Broad Well. Although in the immediate area Woodmancote offers a better selection of 18th-century houses, Dursley is a pleasant, old fashioned sort of place and exploration of its centre is rewarding.

The village of Cam, just to the north of Dursley, still has a single factory producing high quality cloth, mostly for dress uniforms and for snooker table coverings. Cam church, apparently built by Lord Berkeley to save his soul after the murder of Edward II at Berkeley Castle, contains a Jacobean pulpit. The nearby Cam Peak and Cam Long Down are Cotswold outliers, which clearly show their geological formation, the softer rock having eroded around them.

Just to the northwest of Dursley is Stinchcombe Hill, the most westerly point of the Cotswolds. From its summit, Drakestone Point, there are far-reaching views along the escarpment to the Forest of Dean and the River Severn.

DYRHAM MAP REF ST7475

Eight miles (13km) to the north of Bath is Dyrham, a picturesque village bearing a name that is associated with a battle of enormous consequence for Britain. It was on nearby Hinton Hill, in AD 577 that the invading Anglo-Saxons defeated the Britons, forcing them for ever into the mountains of Wales and permitting the capture of the Romano-British cities of Bath, Cirencester and Gloucester.

Dyrham Park was a Tudor house substantially rebuilt at the end of the 17th century for William Blathwayt. Now a National Trust property, it contains magnificent collections of china and Dutch paintings of the period, a reflection of the regular journeys that Blathwayt made to Holland in the company of William III. In the garden is one of the earliest-known greenhouses, while all that remains of the once elaborate water garden in the formal Dutch style is a statue of Neptune.

A herd of fallow deer grazes in the parkland, as they have done since Saxon times, though now the park rejoices in the more naturalistic English style, designed by the great landscape architect Humphry Repton. In 1993 the house was used as a backdrop for the film *Remains of the Day*.

MINCHINHAMPTON

MAP REF SO8700

Overlooking the Stroud Valley on the fringe of the eponymous common, Minchinhampton, one of the most important cloth towns of south Gloucestershire by the 18th century, easily goes unheeded. It was a town of small traders unable to withstand the various crashes that periodically afflicted the industry, and so finally relapsed to a rural calm. Indeed, the church's truncated tower may be explained by the absence of wealthy patrons to replace the decayed spire.

It deserves a look, however, for it is an attractive wool town built around the old Market Square. Here you'll find a 17th-century Market House balanced on stone pillars and the post office residing in a former coaching inn.

The church, just apart from the square, dates back to the 12th century. It contains a particularly fine set of brasses, while the 14th-century south transept contains a stately array of tombs and effigies.

Minchinhampton Common is 580 acres (234ha) of National Trust owned grassland. A wide, windswept expanse of pasture, fringed with the villages of the Frome and Nailsworth valleys, a circumnavigation of the common is rewarding for the views that it reveals.

■ Insight

MINCHINHAMPTON COMMON

After the common was granted to the people of Minchinhampton in the 16th century, any weaver was permitted to enclose land here and build a home. The bulwarks are the remains of an Iron Age fort, and the possible base for the resistance to the Romans led by Caratacus; while Whitefield's Tump is a barrow from where George Whitefield, the Gloucester-born Methodist preacher addressed a 20,000-strong congregation in 1743. During World War I the common was used as an airfield by Australian airmen.

NORTHLEACH MAP REF SP1114

One of the most important of the wool towns in the Middle Ages, Northleach retains something of the flavour of that period, with its market square overlooked by one of the finest wool churches in the Cotswolds. It is all now, fortunately, bypassed by the A40 road, replacing the old coaching route which, in the past, ran through the town. The High Street is an interesting mixture of houses of all periods, some of which, unusually, are half-timbered and most of which reflect the burgage plots that belonged to the merchants of yore.

One of these buildings, just east of the market place, is now Keith Harding's World of Mechanical Music, in what was the old school. This is a fascinating place, a shop as you go in, but beyond it a collection of clocks and mechanical instruments from all over Europe, ranging from barrel organs to pianolas. Entertainingly, many of these are frequently demonstrated, while some of the restored items are for sale.

Behind the square, among a little network of lanes about the old mill, is the most striking building in the town, its wool church which, as it stands, dates from the 15th century. A very fine example of the English Perpendicular style, it is particularly noted for its magnificent south porch, one of the finest in the country. The interior is quite stark but beautifully proportioned and contains the grandest collection of monumental brasses in the Cotswolds, commemorating the medieval wool merchants who brought prosperity to Northleach and whose money was given to build the church.

There are two sets of almshouses, one at Mill End, another at East End. At the western end of the town the High Street meets the Roman Fosse Way. On the other side of the road is an 18th-century building that was originally a prison. The prison was built by Sir William Blackburn according to the ideas of the philanthropist Sir George Onesiphorus Paul, a member of an eminent family of Woodchester clothiers. The courthouse was in use until 1974.

A short drive (or walk) to the northwest is the hamlet of Hampnett, which has an exceptionally interesting Norman church with carved birds on the chancel arch and Victorian stencilling.

PAINSWICK MAP REF SO8609

The 'Queen of the Cotswolds' sits more or less at the point of transition from the northern to the southern Cotswolds. Perched regally at the edge of the steep slopes of the Painswick Valley, the town is a hive of activity about the little network of lanes around the church. It is the most Dickensian in character of the Cotswold villages. Like other important towns in this part of the Cotswolds,

■ Insight

BURGAGE PLOTS

Burgage plots were created to enable the maximum number of shops to line the main street. Northleach Borough was established by the Abbey of St Peter, in Gloucester, in 1226. The annual rents were one shilling (5p) for a burgage plot, 6d (2.5p) for a market stall and 1d for a cottage. These medieval property boundaries can still be traced.

Insight

THE CLIPPING CEREMONY

The Clipping Ceremony at Painswick church has nothing to do with pruning the famous yew trees in the churchyard but derives from the Old English word 'clyppan', meaning to embrace. It takes place on the nearest Sunday to 19 September, in association with the Feast of the Nativity of St Mary. In the afternoon the children involved in the ceremony join hands to form a circle around the church, approach the church and retreat three times as they sing a traditional hymn. A special cake is also baked – known as 'puppy dog pie', it contains a small china dog, a reminder, perhaps, of the pagan origins of the festivity.

Painswick's prosperity reached its peak in the 17th and 18th centuries when the stream below was harnessed to work the mills producing wool cloth. The purity of the water also meant that cloth dyeing became important. The character of the village depends considerably on the fine houses built by the wealthy wool merchants of the era.

But the most striking feature of Painswick is the graceful 17th-century spire of the church. The church itself is mainly 15th-century and contains some interesting monuments, although it is the churchyard for which Painswick is especially noted. There are two reasons for this. The most striking features are the clipped colonnades of yew, which have graced the churchyard since 1792. There are said to be only 99, since the Devil always kills off the hundredth, and indeed, it is now impossible to count them with ease since some have become intertwined with others. The other distinction are table tombs from the 17th and 18th centuries, many of which were carved by a local mason, Joseph Bryan, and his two sons.

Stroll around the heart of the town and along Bisley Street, the original main street and the oldest part of the town. Here you will find the Little Fleece, now a National Trust bookshop in a largely 17th-century house that was built onto the 14th-century Fleece Inn.

Just outside the town, on the Gloucester road, is Painswick Rococo Garden, the landscaped 18th-century garden around Painswick House. It is utterly charming, particularly in early spring when snowdrops flower in abundance. Nearby is Painswick Beacon, site of an Iron Age fort known as Kimsbury Camp and of a golf course, from where there are tremendous views across the plain to Gloucester.

The neighbouring villages of Sheepscombe and Slad are noted for their associations with the *Cider With Rosie* author Laurie Lee.

PRINKNASH MAP REF SO8814

Close to Painswick on the sheltered slopes beneath Cranham Woods is a building which, despite looking like a huge cinema, just about succeeds in blending in with its surroundings, a testament to the use of good building materials, in this case stone from the quarries around Guiting. Prinknash (pronounced 'Prinash'), a Benedictine house, is one of Britain's few abbeys. The 16th-century foundation, a hunting lodge for the abbots of Gloucester, became a manor house and chapel. It was used as his headquarters by Prince Rupert during the Siege of Gloucester and is still visible across the valley. Its location was celebrated by Horace Walpole who, in 1714, described it as 'commanding Elysium'. The last private owner was a Catholic who invited the monks to move here from Caldey Island, off the Welsh coast. The current building was begun in 1939. The abbey is worth visiting for its views and the gardens. The nearby Bird and Deer Park, set in 9 acres (3.6ha) of parkland, is well stocked with birds, goats and deer.

THE SODBURYS MAP REF ST7282

There are in fact three Sodburys – Little, Old and Chipping – scattered around narrow lanes down the Cotswold escarpment, with a remote character that hardly seems Cotswold, and in fact has more in common with the vale. Chipping Sodbury (Chipping, as elsewhere, here means 'market') is the newest of the villages, deliberately established to become a market town in 1227. More recently, J K Rowling, author of the Harry Potter books, was born here. Old Sodbury, the original, has an ancient church and a Bronze to Iron Age encampment above the town from where there are magnificent views.

Little Sodbury is the most interesting of the three. Small as it is, this village has a rich history. Gloucestershire-born scholar William Tyndale (c1494–1536), the translator of the Bible into English, came to the manor house in 1521 as tutor and chaplain. A few years later,

Henry VIII and Anne Boleyn stayed in the house, which has a wonderful 15th-century Great Hall.

The church, dedicated to St Adeline, originally stood next to the manor house but was moved to its present site when urgent repairs had to be carried out. Near the Sodburys is the Somerset, or Hawkesbury, Monument, erected in 1846. This commemorates Lord Edward Somerset, one of the Badminton Beauforts. He served at the Battle of Waterloo with exceptional gallantry for which he received thanks from the government of the day.

■ Visit

CRAFTS IN PAINSWICK
The area around Painswick has strong associations with the Arts and Crafts Movement, and includes the window in the Congregational Church by Morris and Co, the Gyde Almshouses and the public baths, both designed by Sidney Barnsley. Those traditions are carried on today through the Gloucestershire Guild of Craftsmen, the longest-established craft guild in Britain. They have a gallery in Painswick where high quality contemporary work can be found. Events and exhibitions are arranged throughout the year.

■ Visit

ST ADELINE'S CHURCH
The little church of Chipping Sodbury was built in Victorian times on the site of an earlier church, of which only the pulpit (where Tyndale would have preached) remains. It is the only church dedicated to St Adeline, an obscure saint who may have originated from Normandy, possibly indicating a connection between the two places

SOUTH CERNEY & THE COTSWOLD WATER PARK

MAP REF SU0497

South Cerney, 3 miles (4.8km) southeast of Cirencester, is situated on the banks of the Churn, where you will find rows of attractive cottages along Silver Street and Church Lane. The church has a Norman south doorway above which are sculptures reflecting Heaven and Hell, while within are the remains of a 12th-century crucifix, one of the earliest wood carvings in the country.

The old Thames and Severn Canal passes just to the north of the village and walks along the tow-path are possible; but the village is best known nowadays for the series of flooded gravel pits that make up the Cotswold Water Park. Broadly speaking there are two sections, one between Cricklade and Kemble (where South Cerney is situated), the other between Fairford and Lechlade, which provide facilities for nature lovers, birders and sportsmen alike. There are eight nature reserves and the wetlands attract over 20,000 wildfowl, particularly in the winter. The various activities coexist happily on 147 lakes.

THE STROUD VALLEY

For a small area, the Cotswolds reveal remarkable natural diversity, but the Stroud Valley possesses a singular character, much dependent on its depth, narrow base and serpentine course. Stroud itself is at the head of the valley, which runs east close to the Roman city of Cirencester, a number of other valleys feeding it from north and south.

Its character is also dependent upon its history as the manufacturing centre of the Cotswolds, with its fast-flowing streams and the mills that straddled them. Stroud became the centre of the wool industry from the 15th century as cloth supplanted fleece in importance. With industrialisation during the 18th and 19th centuries the valley bristled with mills. There were 150 of them at one time, before decline set in as the industry moved away to Yorkshire, leaving only two companies producing high-quality cloth for dress uniforms.

Stroud is itself spread a little like a cloth over the Cotswold slopes. Of no great beauty, it is nonetheless a bustling town of considerable interest, centred in the area around the High Street, close to which you will find the Shambles, the former meat market, and the Tudor Town Hall. Close by, on George Street, are the handsome 19th-century Subscription Rooms, home to the Tourist Information Centre. The Museum in the Park, which is situated next to the Stratford Park Leisure Centre, offers an excellent insight into the history of the area and displays, among other items, a collection of early lawnmowers (the inventor of the lawnmower, Mr Budding, was from this valley).

There are some good walks to be had along the Stroudwater Canal, once the more successful part of the Thames and Severn Canal system, functioning until 1941, and now being restored.

Southwest of Stroud lies Selsley Common and Selsley, with its church of particular interest for its stained glass by William Morris, Philip Webb, Dante

■ Insight

ARTS AND CRAFTS MOVEMENT

The Arts and Crafts Movement, a London and Cotswold phenomenon, was a 19th-century aesthetic and social movement instigated by the art critic John Ruskin and the artist and poet William Morris as a constructive protest against the mass-produced excesses of the Industrial Revolution. A company, Morris & Co, was established to produce handmade furniture, glass, wallpapers and textiles. It looked to the Middle Ages for its ideal and liked to concentrate on fine materials, solid craftsmanship and expertise, and a certain simplicity of style that was both rustic and courtly, of universal appeal. Later, in 1888, Morris helped the artist and designer C R Ashbee to found the Guild and School of Arts and Crafts, but production costs led to its early demise. However, some of the designs, particularly for textiles and wallpaper, remain popular and the tradition of quality workmanship continues to inspire craftsmen in the area.

Gabriel Rossetti, Edward Burne-Jones and Ford Madox Brown. Just farther west, near Stonehouse, is one of the area's pre-industrial legacies, the 13th-century Frocester Tithe Barn, believed to be one of the finest in England.

To the east of Stroud is Chalford, its houses on steep lanes and along terraces and shelves of the north slope of the valley. A legacy of the Industrial Revolution, its houses were built by the clothiers and merchants making their fortune during the 18th and 19th centuries and by weavers working first from home and later at the mills that still line the Thames and Severn Canal. It has two chuches that contain work produced by members of the Arts and Crafts Movement.

The Thames and Severn Canal, today a restoration project, was one of those great Victorian enterprises that was magnificent in conception but almost redundant by the time of its realisation. Completed in 1789, to facilitate trade between the two rivers that were also important commercial waterways, the number of locks, problems with the size of the 2.17-mile (3.5km) Sapperton Tunnel and a shortage of water engendered constant problems. Other, better, canals and the arrival of the railways put paid to it and the last recorded journey was made in 1911. The two temple-like tunnel portals are visible at Coates and Daneway where the pubs, built for the boatmen, still function. A stroll along the old canal is recommended, as indeed is a visit to the village of Sapperton, the home of Ernest Gimson and the Barnsley brothers, of the Arts and Crafts Movement.

Just to the north of Chalford is Bisley village, with pubs and a church that has a dramatic spire and, in the church-yard, a unique 'Poor Soul's Light', a 13th-century structure that contained candles lit during masses for the poor.

South of Stroud at Woodchester, is the site of a Roman villa with a magnificent Orpheus mosaic buried in the churchyard. Woodchester Mansion lies south of Woodchester on the road to Dursley. It is a fascinating place to visit as the house was abandoned by its builders in the mid 1870s before it could be completed. It is preserved in the state it was left.

To the south, just outside Nailsworth, is the fascinating Dunkirk Mill, where a massive overshot waterwheel can be seen, together with a well-presented history of the local textile industry.

TETBURY MAP REF ST8993

This is a small, tranquil market town of some charm, set among the broader slopes of the southern Cotswolds, on a promontory overlooking a tributary of the River Avon.

By the 18th century Tetbury was one of the most important cloth market towns of south Gloucestershire. Its main streets radiate from the still impressive market square, dominated by the 17th-century Town Hall or Market House, resting on three rows of tubby Etruscan pillars, but reduced by one storey in 1817. The square is also noted for the Snooty Fox Hotel, the former White Hart. It was rebuilt by the designer of Westonbirt House with entertainment for the Beaufort Hunt in mind.

The road next to the Snooty Fox leads to Chipping Steps and the site of the old livestock market, surrounded by some handsome 18th- and 19th-century houses and the Old Priory. The road continues down to the foot of Gumstool Hill, the scene for the annual Woolsack Races on Millennium Green on Spring Bank Holiday Monday.

South from the square, along Church Street, is the magnificent St Mary's Church, rebuilt in Gothic style in the late 18th century. The spire is 186 feet (57m) tall. The interior, lit by Perpendicular-style windows, is coolly elegant. Rows of box pews, with their own entries from the ambulatories, are presided over by panelled galleries and two splendid chandeliers. The church is the home of the Tetbury Heritage Display.

Tetbury has an unusual museum, at the western end of Long Street, which runs west out of Market Square. The Tetbury Heritage Centre is housed in the cells of the Old Court House and displays police memorabilia such as uniforms on loan from Gloucestershire Constabulary.

Just over a mile (1.6km) to the northwest of Tetbury is Chavenage, a delightful manor. There is a fine collection of 17th-century tapestries. The chapel, with an early Norman font found in an estate barn, is close by. About 4 miles (6.4km) to the northeast, stands Rodborough Manor, an impressive example of a house built in the traditional Arts and Crafts style.

Three miles (4.8km) southwest of Tetbury is magnificent Westonbirt Arboretum, where more than 16,000 trees thrive in 600 acres (243ha) of glade and 17 miles (27.2km) of footpaths. The Arboretum was started in 1829 by Sir Robert Holford of Westonbirt House designed by Lewis Vulliamy, who also designed the Snooty Fox in Tetbury and London's Dorchester House (demolished to make way for the hotel).

■ Activity

RODBOROUGH COMMON

Rodborough Common is just to the south-west of Stroud. A good place for walking, the common is also the site of Rodborough Fort, built in 1764 as a pleasure-house by George Hawker, a local dyer. It was rebuilt in Victorian style in 1870.

ULEY & OWLPEN MAP REF ST7898

Uley is a large and pretty village of 18th-century houses scuttling down the hillside into a deep valley, which became prosperous through wool dyeing. There is still a functioning brewery, while the Old Crown is a fine pub. Uley Bury overlooks the town – it is a classic site for a hill-fort, a flat 32-acre (13ha) plateau surrounded by steep slopes.

North of Uley, towards Frocester Hill, is Hetty Pegler's Tump – the unusual name comes from the 17th-century landowner's wife. This 180-foot (55m) Neolithic barrow, surrounded by a stone wall, has a long central chamber that can be entered, with some discomfort, by obtaining the key from a nearby cottage. It may be wise to take a torch. East of Uley, within striking distance by foot, is Owlpen Manor, a beautifully sited and very picturesque 15th-century manor house restored in the 1920s, displaying a good collection of Arts and Crafts furniture. Close by is the 19th-century church and 18th-century mill.

About a mile (1.6km) east of Owlpen is a most tranquil garden at Kingscote called Matara. Eastern and Western ideas of garden design are blended to produce a very restful place.

WOTTON-UNDER-EDGE
MAP REF ST7593

Wotton-under-Edge is perhaps one of the most interesting small towns in the Cotswolds. In the Middle Ages Wotton was an important wool town entitled to hold markets and fairs and the Chipping, part of which is now a car park, was the site for them. The old fire station in the Chipping is now an interesting heritage centre, showing the history of the town and the surrounding area. From the Chipping, Market Street leads past the Star Inn and the Town Hall, to a junction with High Street and Long Street.

On the corner of Market Street and High Street there is the smart red-brick Tolsey House, granted to the town in 1595 by the Countess of Warwick to serve as a market court. Overlooking the High Street from the other side of Haw Street is the old police station.

Long Street, the main shopping thoroughfare, which is lined with an array of architectural styles. A stroll along Orchard Street on the right will bring you to the school where Isaac Pitman, inventor of shorthand, taught. At the end of Long Street turn left into Church Street, opposite the 17th-century Falcon Inn. On the right is a row of delightful almshouses, built in 1638. If you choose, go into the courtyard and visit the little chapel, lit by a pair of depictive stained-glass windows.

Church Street then crosses over Old Town to Culverhay, to the 18th-century Church Hall, former home to the Blue Coat Church of England School, and the entrance to the parish church, consecrated in 1283, though most of the building is 15th century. Beyond the churchyard is Potters Pond where the Ram Inn, dating from before 1350, is thought to be the oldest building here.

Just over a mile (2.4km) to the east at Ozleworth stands Newark Park, an unusual 16th-century house built as a hunting lodge, with magnificent views across the countryside.

From Bradford-on-Avon along the Kennet & Avon Canal

The Kennet and Avon Canal is ideal for cyclists and passes through picturesque countryside. You can turn around at the riverside pub at Bathampton although the locks you pass on the way into Bath are well worth seeing.

Route Directions

1 Leaving the station car park, turn right along the main road in the direction of Frome. Continue past a mini-roundabout to the Canal Tavern and Lock Inn Café. Go between them to join the towpath and follow it past Grange Farm with its massive 600-year-old tithe barn. The River Avon runs below to the right, containing Barton Farm Country Park's picnic and wildlife areas within the intervening spit of land. Beyond a gate, continue beside the canal to Avoncliff.

2 The canal now makes an abrupt turn across the Avon Valley, carried above both the river and railway on an imposing aqueduct. Do not cross, but at a sign to Dundas just before, drop steeply right towards the Cross Guns pub, then double back left underneath the bridge, climbing left to gain the opposite tow path. Tacked along the wooded valley, the waterway runs pleasantly on, harbouring an assortment of

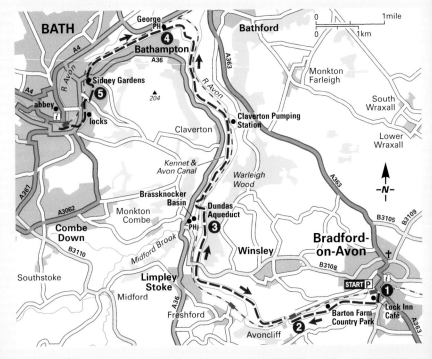

ducks, coots and moorhens. Turning a corner opposite Limpley Stoke, pass beneath a road bridge, then look out on the left for a glimpse of a viaduct taking the A36 across the Midford Brook valley.

3 Another sharp turn heralds the Dundas Aqueduct, beyond which is the last remnant of the Somerset Coal Canal. The track just before it leads to Brassknocker Basin, with a small exhibition. The route, however, continues ahead, signed 'Bath and Claverton', behind a maintenance building and a derrick and onto the opposite bank. A mile (1.2km) further on, immediately beyond a bridge, a track drops across the railway to the river where there is a restored pump house (Claverton Pumping Station), built in 1813. There are views to Bathford and Batheaston as you pedal the final 1.75 miles (2.8km) to Bathampton and The George.

4 To extend the ride, continue beside the canal, the eastern suburbs of Bath rising on the opposite side of the valley. Eventually the city comes into view. There are a couple of short tunnels to pass through at Sidney Gardens, where you should dismount. Between them, two ornate cast-iron bridges span the canal, which, together with the elaborate façade of the second tunnel beneath Cleveland House, were added to placate the owners of Sidney Park, who disapproved of the cargo barges passing through their land.

5 Emerging below Cleveland House, the tow path doubles back onto the opposite bank, passes former warehouses, now a marina, and rises to a road. Taking care, diagonally cross and drop back to the tow path, here negotiating steps. Beyond, the canal falls through a succession of locks, the path periodically rising to cross a couple of roads and a track before meeting the River Avon. To explore Bath, carry on a little further by the river to emerge on the road beside Churchill Bridge in the city centre. As the city is busy, it is wise to secure your bikes while you wander around. The return is back the way you came, but remember you have to climb steps to the road at Bathwick Hill and dismount through the tunnels at Sidney Gardens, or you can return by train.

Route facts

DISTANCE/TIME
20 miles (32.2km) 4h
SHORTER ROUTE
15 miles (24.1km) 3h

MAP OS Explorer 155 Bristol & Bath & 156 Chippenham & Bradford-on-Avon

START Bradford-on-Avon railway station (pay car park); grid ref: ST 825606

TRACKS Gravel tow path, short section on road

GETTING TO THE START
Bradford-on-Avon is only 5 miles (8km) southeast of Bath and lies on the A363 to Trowbridge. Park at the railway station, from where the ride begins.

CYCLE HIRE The Lock Inn Café, 48 Frome Road, Bradford-on-Avon. Tel: 01225 868068

THE PUB The George, Mill Lane, Bathampton. Tel: 01225 425079

❶ Care through town; unguarded canal tow paths shared with pedestrians; blind approaches to bridges; dismount in tunnels; steps on approaching Bath.

Corsham and Corsham Park

This walk explores Corsham, a fine architectural treasure of a town where the 15th-century Flemish gabled cottages and baroque-pedimented 17th-century Hungerford Almshouses mix with larger Georgian residences. The walk continues through adjacent Corsham Park, landscaped by 'Capability' Brown.

Route Directions

1 Turn left out of the car park, then left again along Post Office Lane to reach the High Street. Turn left, pass the tourist information centre and turn right into Church Street. Pass the impressive entrance to the privately owned Corsham Court, on your left, and then enter St Bartholomew's churchyard.

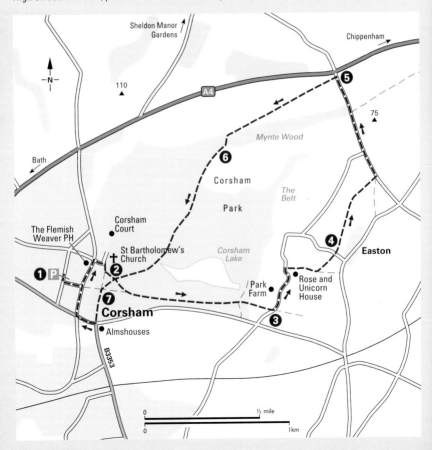

2 Follow the path left to a gate and walk ahead to join the main path across Corsham Park. Turn left and walk along the south side of the park, passing Corsham Lake, to reach a stile and gate. Keep straight on along a fenced path beside a track to reach a kissing gate and proceed across a field to a stile and lane.

3 Turn left, pass Park Farm, a splendid stone farmhouse, on your left and shortly take the waymarked footpath right along a drive to pass Rose and Unicorn House. Cross a stile and follow the right-hand field-edge to a stile, then bear half left to a stone stile in the field corner. Ignore the path arrowed right and head straight across the field to a further stile and lane.

4 Take the footpath opposite, bearing half left to a stone stile to the left of a cottage. Maintain direction, passing to the right of a spring and go through a field entrance to follow the path along the left-hand side of a field to a stile in the corner. Turn left along the road for 0.5 mile (800m) to reach the A4.

5 Go through the gate in the wall on your left and follow the worn path right, across the centre of parkland pasture to a metal kissing gate. Proceed ahead to reach a kissing gate on the edge of woodland. Follow the wide path to a further gate and bear half right to a stile.

6 Keep ahead on a worn path across the parkland and along the field-edge to a gate. Continue to a further gate with fine views right to Corsham Court. Follow the path right along the field-edge, then where it curves right, bear left to join the path beside the churchyard wall to a stile.

7 Turn left down the avenue of trees to a gate and the town centre, noting the stone almshouses on your left. Turn right along Lacock Road and then right again along the pedestrianised High Street. Turn left back along Post Office Lane to the car park.

Route facts

DISTANCE/TIME
4 miles (6.4km) 2h

MAP OS Explorer 156 Chippenham & Bradford-on-Avon

START Corsham: long stay car park in Newlands Lane; grid ref: ST 871704

TRACKS Field paths and country lanes, 10 stiles

GETTING TO THE START
Corsham is just 4 miles (6.4km) southwest of Chippenham, where the B3353 meets the A4. The walk begins from the town's long stay car park on Newland's Road, which is signposted from the main road.

THE PUB The Flemish Weaver, Corsham. Tel: 01249 701929

❶ Suitability: an easy walk although care should be taken along the road section.

■ TOURIST INFORMATION CENTRES

Bath
Abbey Chambers, Abbey Churchyard. Tel: 0906 711 2000; www.visitbath.co.uk

Cirencester
Corinium Museum, Park Street. Tel: 01285 654180

Painswick
The Library, Stroud Road. Tel: 01452 813552

Stroud
Subscription Rooms, George Street. Tel: 01453 760960

Tetbury
33 Church Street.
Tel: 01666 503552

■ PLACES OF INTEREST

Barnsley House Gardens
Barnsley. Tel: 01285 740000;
www.barnsleyhouse.com

Bath Abbey Heritage Vaults
Tel: 01225 4224628

Bath Postal Museum
27 Northgate Street.
Tel: 01225 460333; www.
bathpostalmuseum.org

Beckford's Tower and Museum
Lansdown Road, Bath.
Tel: 01225 460705; www.bath-preservation-trust.org.uk

Bristol Aero Collection
Kemble. Tel: 01285 771204
www.bristolaero.com

Building of Bath Museum
The Vineyards, Bath. Tel:
01225 333895; www.bath-preservation-trust.org.uk

Buscot Park
Buscot. Tel: 0845 3453387;
www.buscot-park.com

Cerney House Gardens
North Cerney.
Tel: 01285 831300; www.
cerneygardens.com

Chavenage House
Tetbury. Tel: 01666 502329;
www.chavenage.com

Chedworth Roman Villa
Yanworth, near Cheltenham.
Tel: 01242 890256; www.
chedworthromanvilla.com

Compton Cassey Gallery
Compton Cassey House, near
Withington. Tel: 01242 890224;
www.jonathanpoole.co.uk

Corinium Museum
Park Street, Cirencester.
Tel: 01285 655611; www.
cotswold.gov.uk/go/museum

Dunkirk Mill Centre
Stroud. Tel: 01453 766273;
www.stroud-textile.org.uk

Dyrham Park
Dyrham. Tel: 0117 9372501;
www.nationaltrust.org.uk

Fashion Museum
Bennett Street, Bath.
Tel: 01225 477173; www.
museumofcostume.co.uk

Herschel Museum of Astronomy
19 New King Street, Bath.
Tel: 01225 446865; www.bath-preservation-trust.org.uk

Holburne Museum of Art
Great Pulteney Street, Bath.
Closed until spring 2011.
www.bath.ac.uk/holburne

Jane Austen Centre
Gay Street, Bath.
Tel: 01225 443000;
www.janeausten.co.uk

Matara Gardens
Kingscote Park, Kingscote.
Tel: 01453 861050;
www.matara.co.uk

Museum in the Park
Stratford Park, Stroud.
Tel: 01453 763394; www.
museuminthepark.org.uk

Number 1, Royal Crescent
Bath. Tel: 01225 428126;
www.bath-preservation-trust.
org.uk

Newark Park
Ozleworth, Wotton-under-
Edge. Tel: 01793 817666;
www.nationaltrust.org.uk

Owlpen Manor
Uley.Tel: 01453 860261;
www.owlpen.com

Painswick Rococo Garden
Gloucester Road, Painswick.
Tel: 01452 813204;
www.rococogarden.co.uk

Prinknash Bird and Deer Park
Tel: 01452 812727;
www.thebirdpark.co.uk

Roman Baths Museum
Stall Street, Bath.
Tel: 01225 477785;
www.romanbaths.co.uk

Ruskin Mill College Gallery
Old Bristol Road,
Nailsworth.
Tel: 01453 832571;
www.ruskin-mill.org.uk

Tetbury Heritage Centre
The Old Courthouse, 63 Long
Street. Tel: 01666 837500;
www.tetbury.gov.uk

Thermae Bath Spa
Hot Bath Street, Bath.
Tel: 01225 331234;
www.thermaebathspa.com

Victoria Art Gallery
Bridge Street, Bath.
Tel: 01225 477233;
www.victoriagal.org

Westonbirt Arboretum
Tel: 01666 880554.
Open all year, daily.

Woodchester Mansion
Nympsfield.
Tel: 01453 861541; www.
woodchestermansion.org.uk

**Wotton-under-Edge
Heritage Centre**
The Chipping, Wotton-under-
Edge. Tel: 01453 521541;
www.wottonheritage.com

■ FOR CHILDREN
Bath Treasure Hunt on Foot
Tel: 01904 491549;
www.huntfun.co.uk

Butts Farm Visitor Centre
Nr South Cerney.
Tel: 01285 869414;
www.buttsfarmshop.com

Norwood Farm
Bath Road, Norton St Philip.
Tel: 01373 834356

**Prinknash Bird
and Deer Park**
Near Cranham.
Tel: 01452 812727;
www.thebirdpark.co.uk

■ SHOPPING
Bath
Farmers' Market Sat,
Green Park Station.

Cirencester
Farmers' Market second and
fourth Sat; Charter Market
Mon and Fri, both held in
Market Place.

Dursley
Farmers' Market second
and fourth Sat.

Fairford
Market, Wed.

Stroud
Farmers' Market Sat,
Market Hall.

Tetbury
Market, Wed.

LOCAL SPECIALITIES
Crafts
New Brewery Arts,
Cirencester.
Tel: 01285 657181; www.
newbreweryarts.org.uk

Pottery
Lansdown Pottery,
Stroud.
Tel: 01453 753051;
www.lansdownpottery.co.uk

■ PERFORMING ARTS
Cotswold Playhouse
Parliament Street, Stroud.
Tel: 01453 760960; www.
cotswoldplayhouse.co.uk

Theatre Royal
Sawclose, Bath.
Tel: 01225 448844;
www.theatreroyal.org.uk

■ OUTDOOR ACTIVITIES
BOAT TRIPS
Bath
The Penny Lane, North
Parade Bridge.
Tel: 01225 303434;
www.prideofbath.com

COUNTRY PARKS
Cotswold Water Park
South Cerney
Tel: 01793 752413;
www.waterpark.org

CYCLE HIRE
Cirencester
Ride 24/7, 6 The Woolmarket.
Tel: 01285 642247;
www.ride-247.co.uk

■ ANNUAL EVENTS
& CUSTOMS
Badminton
Badminton Horse Trials, May.

Bath
Literature Festival, Feb/Mar;
Music Festival, May/Jun;
Children's Literature Festival
Sep/Oct;
Mozartfest. Nov.

Cirencester
Cotswold Country Fair, Jul.

Fairford
Royal International Air Tattoo,
Jul.

Gatcombe
Horse Trials, Jul or Aug.

Painswick
Church Clipping Ceremony,
late Sep.

Tea Rooms

The Pump Room
Stall Street, Bath BA1 1LZ
Tel: 01225 444477;
www.searcys.co.uk/
thepumproom/
The splendid afternoon tea is
impeccably served to the
strains of classical music
in the background in the
elegant surroundings of
the Pump Room.

Woodruff's Organic Café
High Street, Stroud GL5 1JA
Tel: 01453 759195; www.
woodruffesorganiccafe.co.uk
Organic, locally sourced and
seasonal food makes up the
menu at this friendly café.
Mainly vegetarian, but with
several fish dishes on offer,
the selection of meals is very
enticing. Delicious cakes.

Tollgate Tea Shop
Oldfield Gatehouse,
Dyrham Park SN14 8ER
Tel: 01225 891585;
www.tollgateteashop.co.uk
Visit this stone building with
arched windows for teas
served in a welcoming
atmosphere. No artificial
ingredients are used in their
excellent cakes and scones.

Ruskin Mill
Old Bristol Road, Nailsworth
GL6 0LA. Tel: 01453 837500
www.ruskin-mill.org.uk

Make time, when visiting this
vibrant art and craft centre, to
enjoy tea with organic cake
before a stroll round the
gardens and the ponds.

Hobbs House
4 George Street, Nailsworth
GL6 0AG. Tel: 01453 839396;
www.hobbshousebakery.co.uk
This innovative café, which is
one of Rick Stein's Food
Heroes, sells an amazing
range of breads and
patisserie using locally
sourced ingredients.

Pubs

The New Inn at Coln
Coln St Aldwyns GL7 5AN
Tel: 01285 750651;
www.new-inn.co.uk
One of the prettiest villages in
the Cotswolds is home to this
attractive inn. Eat in the bar,
or in the flower-filled
courtyard, or, for a superb
meal, try the restaurant.

The Green Dragon Inn
Cockleford, Cowley
GL53 9NW
Tel: 01242 870271;
www.green-dragon-inn.co.uk
Tucked away in a small
hamlet, this 17th-century
stone inn offers peace and
relaxation. One of the bars has
work by Robert Thompson,
with his famous trademark
mice carved into the furniture

and fittings. The menu here is
extensive, and there are also
good wines.

The Crown Inn
Frampton Mansell GL6 8JG
Tel: 01285 760601; www.
thecrowninn-cotswolds.co.uk
This old inn, in the Golden
Valley, is full of low beams
and has cosy open fireplaces.
In warm weather, there is
plenty of seating in the
garden. Fresh, local food is
served in the restaurant and
in the three inviting bars.

The Weighbridge Inn
Minchinhampton GL6 9AL
Tel: 01453 832520;
www.2in1pub.co.uk
This former weighbridge is
full of local memorabilia. It is
most famous, however, for its
2 in 1 pies, with home-made
cauliflower cheese as one
part and the meat or fish
filling of your choice.

The Bell at Sapperton
Sapperton GL7 6LE
Tel: 01285 760298;
www.foodatthebell.co.uk
The 300-year-old bell is
elegant in an understated way
– all stone walls and fresh
flowers on scrubbed tables.
Dishes include home-made
ravioli with Portland crab and
braised pork in red wine and
balsamic sherry.

Eastern Cotswolds

The distinctive character of the Cotswolds spills over into the surrounding counties of Gloucestershire, Oxfordshire and Warwickshire, where charming villages of honeyed limestone can be found amid rolling pastures. Some of these unspoiled villages are described in the text on the following pages, and others, particularly those of Warwickshire, are included in Car Tour 1.

9 Walk start point

3 Cycle start point

BURFORD

KELMSCOTT MANOR GARDENS

Unmissable attractions

Like the other parts of the Cotswolds, this eastern area, which falls mostly within Oxfordshire, has many charming villages (with equally charming names), such as Minster Lovell and Chipping Norton. Two of these pretty villages, Burford and Chipping Norton, have circular mapped walks that start in the village centre. Also in this area is magnificent Blenheim Palace, a World Heritage Site, which has vast gardens and is famous as the birthplace of Winston Churchill. Kelmscott Manor, on the edge of Kelmscott, is a 16th-century, limestone farmhouse set in lovely gardens.

1

1 Blenheim Palace
The extensive grounds of Blenheim Palace are a perfect setting for the superb building, designed by Sir John Vanbrugh.

2 Dovecote, Minster Lovell
The circular medieval dovecote near Minister Lovell Hall has been well maintained, revealing its intricate construction.

3 Kelmscott Manor
William Morris, founder of the Arts and Crafts Movement, lived at the manor for 25 years. The property is a showcase for the ideals and work of the movement.

BURFORD MAP REF SP2512

Just off the main Oxford road, Burford is all but invisible to passing motorists. Drive north from the roundabout, however, and almost immediately, from the brow of the ridge, Burford slips away before you in a sedate cascade of handsome inns and charming cottages. The wide main street, lined with shops and pubs, passes the church to the right before crossing the Windrush on a medieval bridge of 1322, by the old mill.

Burford's prosperity over the centuries has depended on three factors – wool, quarrying, and coaching. There were burgesses here in the 13th century and the town grew rapidly to become an important wool centre.

The nearby quarries at the Barringtons, Upton and especially Taynton produced some of the most notable stone in the Cotswolds. Much of that stone was used in the construction of some of England's finest buildings – Blenheim Palace, St Paul's Cathedral and various Oxford colleges. The Barringtons also produced the Strongs, a family of masons – Sir Thomas Strong was Christopher Wren's master mason in the construction of St Paul's

Cathedral. Another eminent family of masons, the Kempsters, came from Upton and Burford.

A fillip for Burford came with the dawn of the coaching era from the 18th century, when the town was an important stop on the route to Oxford and London. This, however, came to an end with the railway, which happened to bypass Burford.

Burford is a delight to stroll about. While the High Street is the main thoroughfare, Sheep Street to the west, and Witney Street and Church Lane to the east, have much to offer. Along Sheep Street there are some very fine inns – the Bay Tree Hotel and the Lamb Inn (the old brewery next door houses the Tourist Information Centre) – while Witney Street boasts perhaps the finest building in the town, the 17th-century Great House, possibly built by the local mason Christopher Kempster. From Witney Street, Guildenford leads to Church Lane where a row of lovely almshouses, founded in 1457, are close to St John the Baptist church.

The 15th-century parish church is impressive. Among the chapels and monuments, perhaps the finest is the one erected in 1628 to Sir Lawrence Tanfield, Lord Chief Baron of the Exchequer to James I. Another fine memorial, to Edmund Harman, barber-surgeon to Henry VIII, includes the first representation in Britain of Amazonian Indians from the New World. On the rim of the font the autograph of a Leveller, one of 340 Roundhead mutineers kept here for three days during the Civil War, is inscribed: 'Anthony Sedley prisner

■ Visit

ROYAL APPOINTMENT

Burford was also famous for its saddlery business. This was in part, at least, a result of the proximity of the Bibury races, which used to take place on the course near Aldsworth. Burford saddles received an unspoken royal appointment as a result of the visits of Charles II and his mistress Nell Gwynn who used to stay here when the races were on.

1649' (sic). From the High Street, near the bridge, Priory Lane takes you past the handsome Elizabethan Priory, and round to Falkland Hall, built in 1558.

Back on the High Street, on the corner of Sheep Street, is the pillared Tolsey, a Tudor house where wool merchants used to meet and which now houses a museum of considerable interest. Further down is the wide arch of the old George Hotel where Charles II used to stay with Nell Gwynn and which later became an important coaching inn. Their son was created Earl of Burford.

Three miles (4.8km) south of Burford are the Cotswold Wildlife Park and Gardens, set in the grounds of a 19th-century mansion. The varied collection consists of animals from all over the world, with tropical birds, reptiles, an aquarium, insect house and children's farmyard. The gardens, including tropical plants are attractions in their own right and are continually improving.

CHARLBURY MAP REF SP3519

Here is a town that is unexpected in a number of ways. This area of the Cotswolds hides its villages well in its folds and Charlbury is a small, busy town that looks across the Evenlode valley in happy isolation towards Wychwood Forest. It seems to be self-sufficient, more or less, with a large number of shops, inns and a railway station (designed by Isambard Kingdom Brunel). Although Charlbury was a sheep town in the past, it was also renowned as a centre of glove manufacture. At the height of its prosperity, in the mid-19th century,

■ Insight

SIMON WYSDOM
Opposite the almshouses are the old buildings of Burford Grammar School, founded in 1577 by a wealthy cloth merchant, Simon Wysdom. He was also responsible for the construction of the Weavers' Cottages, which are grouped near the medieval bridge.

■ Insight

BURFORD BAIT
In the days immediately following the opening of the turnpikes, when Burford was an important coaching town, its inns competed with each other for travellers' custom. 'Burford Bait' was the name given to the famously large meals they provided, probably based on venison poached from Wychwood Forest.

more than 1,000 people were employed in the industry.

Behind the main street is a small green, the Playing Close, which is surrounded by handsome villas and cottages, and solid iron railings looking across to a Jacobean-style drinking fountain at one end.

Charlbury's church, on the other side of the main street, is largely Perpendicular in style, with Norman pillars and arches on the north side, but otherwise with a rather Victorian interior. The town museum in Market Street is dedicated to the traditional crafts and industries of the area. Beyond the River Evenlode is Cornbury Park, a gift from Elizabeth I to Robert Dudley. A pleasant walk can be had through the forested grounds of this

Insight

LITERARY ASSOCIATIONS

Finstock, a couple of miles south of Charlbury, has several literary associations. The great poet T S Eliot was baptised into the church here in 1927, while the novelist Barbara Pym, who died in 1980, lived here for the last eight years of her life.

Insight

CHURCHILL

Just 3 miles (4.8km) southwest of Chipping Norton, and close to Stow-on-the-Wold is the village of Churchill, the birthplace of Warren Hastings, the first Governor-General of India. It was also the birthplace of William Smith, 'the Father of English Geology', who produced the first geological map of England. Their stories are well told in the Churchill and Sarsden Heritage Centre in the Old Church which also contains village records and maps dating back to the 17th century.

largely 17th-century house, which will also take you across the approach bridge built in 1689. A National Nature Reserve forms part of the land and this, with the house, is not open to the public.

Ditchley Park, west of Charlbury, is only occasionally open to the public by appointment. The fine 18th-century mansion was built for the 2nd Earl of Lichfield by James Gibbs, while the landscaping is by 'Capability' Brown. The grounds consist of a 300-acre (121ha) park, a lake, temples and woodland. The house was the historic meeting place of Winston Churchill and the US Secretary of Defense during the Second World War.

CHIPPING NORTON

MAP REF SP3127

This busy market town, the highest in Oxfordshire at 646 feet (197m), is distinguished at its outskirts by the large Victorian tweed mill, now converted to flats, that sits in a fold to the west of the town. The Bliss Tweed Mill, built in 1872 by the Lancashire architect George Woodhouse, closed in 1980 and is an unusual reminder, in the Cotswolds, of the Industrial Revolution; and yet there is something disconcertingly memorable about this example of the Victorian age.

The heart of Chipping Norton is the Market Square which is dominated by the 19th-century Town Hall, with its Tuscan-style portico. Opposite the Town Hall steps is the museum, which has displays on the town's history. Around the town you'll find a varied collection of shops, hotels and houses dating back to the 17th century, though most are 18th-century – a testimony to former prosperity based on the wool trade.

From the square, the town slopes down Church Street past a row of almshouses dating back to 1640 towards St Mary's, a Perpendicular church containing some fine brasses and impressive tombs. Its most unusual feature is the hexagonal porch with a vaulted ceiling. Behind the church are the motte and bailey earthworks that show that the town was already of some importance in the Norman period.

In Middle Row look out for the 16th-century Guildhall. Chipping Norton is one of the few towns in the area blessed with a theatre, which is particularly well known for its pantomimes.

The Leach & Coln Valleys

Many Cotswold villages, content in their anonymity tucked away off the tourist trail, offer a quiet escape from hectic modern life. This pleasant ride meanders through villages such as these, crossing the gently rolling downs between the pretty Coln and Leach valleys. The route starts in the picturesque village of Coln St Aldwyns surrounded by pastureland and close to the hamlet of Hatherop.

Route Directions

1 The crossroads in the middle of Coln St Aldwyns is marked by a sturdy spreading chestnut tree. Begin the ride along the lane signed to Quenington and Fairford, passing The New Inn. Leaving the village, cycle over the River Coln and climb to a crossroads at the edge of Quenington. Go left onto Fowlers Hill and drop back into the valley, following signs to Southrop and Lechlade as you bend past a junction to re-cross the Coln. After a bit of a pull, the lane rises over open down, and follows the line of an ancient salt way. Pedal for 2.5 miles (4km), following signs for Southrop past junctions, before losing height to a 'Give Way' junction.

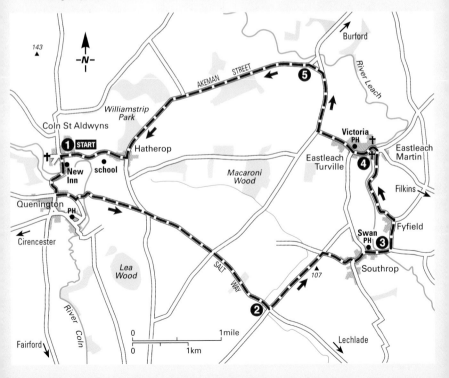

2 Go left, gaining height along a gentle fold in the rolling hillside. Stay with the main lane as it later turns to rise over the hill, winding down on the other side into Southrop. Carry on past the village hall and the Swan, the street slotted between high-kerbed pavements and now signed to Filkins.

3 After dropping away and crossing the second river of the journey, the Leach, turn off left to Fyfield and Eastleach. Keep left again as the lane splits at Fyfield, following the gently rising valley to Eastleach. There are two separately named halves to the village and the lane ends at a junction by the church in Eastleach Martin. Go left, and re-cross the Leach to enter the neighbouring parish, swinging left again beneath a massive willow tree, from which a track leads off to Eastleach Turville's church.

4 The main lane winds on past the village cross and then a row of almshouses to reach a junction below The Victoria pub. Keep ahead, the way signed 'Hatherop and Burford', climbing shortly to a second junction where you should go right in the direction of Burford and Westwell. Undulate onwards across open hills that are interspersed with clumps of copse. Stay left at successive turnings to curve above the higher reaches of the Leach valley. The signs should now be directing you to Hatherop and Coln St Aldwyns.

5 For 1.25 miles (2km), the way follows the course of Akeman Street, a Roman road, passing a turn off signed to Dean Farm before breaking away from the line of the ancient thoroughfare into Hatherop. At a junction, go right towards Coln St Aldwyns, winding down to leave the village past Hatherop School. It is then only a short ride back to the start point at Coln St Aldwyns.

Route facts

DISTANCE/TIME 11.25 miles (26.9km) 2h30

MAP OS Explorer OL45 The Cotswolds

START Coln St Aldwyns; grid ref: SP 145052

TRACKS Minor lanes

GETTING TO THE START
The small village of Coln St Aldwyns nestles in the Coln Valley some 8 miles (12.9km) east of Cirencester. The nearest town is Fairford on the A417, just over 2 miles (3.2km) to the south along the vale. Park in a cul-de-sac at the centre of the village.

THE PUB The Swan, Southrop. Tel: 01367 850205

❶ Care on the narrow lanes is required

■ Insight

QUARRY WORKERS
The last people to work some of the quarries in the Filkins' area, before they were reopened by George Swinford in 1929, were French prisoners of war from the Napoleonic Wars.

FAIRFORD MAP REF SP1501

Fairford is most often thought of in connection with the supersonic aircraft *Concorde*, which had its maiden flight at the military airfield here. Every year in July the Royal International Air Tattoo is held at RAF Fairford. But Fairford is more than an airfield. Located on the River Coln and the A417, Fairford is another of those towns that has a busy lowland feel, which does not seem to be entirely characteristic of the Cotswolds.

The focal point of the village is its magnificent late Perpendicular Church of St Mary, largely rebuilt in the early 1490s by John Tame and his son Edmund, the most influential of Fairford's medieval wool merchants. The parish church is dominated by a central tower supported by massive pillars within; but the spectacular medieval stained-glass windows are its greatest glory. They are the only complete set in the country, and narrate the highlights of the Biblical story. They are most likely the work of the Flanders craftsman, Barnard Flower, whom Henry VIII employed to make the windows of King's College Chapel, Cambridge and the Lady Chapel, Westminster Abbey, and who was almost certainly helped by English and Dutch craftsmen. The great west window, in particular, which shows the Last Judgement, is of riveting, luminous beauty. Not to be missed either are the amusing carved misericords underneath the choir stalls. In the churchyard are buried two distinguished locals – Valentine Strong, of the eminent family of stone quarriers of Taynton; and Tiddles, the church cat.

The church overlooks the green water meadows and the old mill by a picturesque bridge. From the church a pleasant circuit is possible and will bring you back to the main street. Most of the houses that line the street are 17th or 18th century and, along with the many inns, are a reminder of Fairford's role as a coaching town. John Keble, the 19th-century church reformer, was born at Keble House, on the north side of the road at the east end of the town.

To the north are the picturesque twin villages of Eastleach Turville and Eastleach Martin, which are separated by the River Leach.

FILKINS MAP REF SP2304

This is a quiet Cotswold village that has a distinctly bypassed feel. Its cottages are distinguished for their solid craftsmanship rather than their beauty, and their story can be read in an entertaining book, *Jubilee Boy*, (on sale at the woollen mill, among other places) by an ancient local resident, George Swinford. He worked as a foreman on the estate belonging to the British statesman, Sir Stafford Cripps, and has also given his name to the Swinford Museum in the village.

The village is best known, however, for its working woollen-weaving factory, one of the last, if not the last, in the Cotswolds, a rather poignant fact when it is considered that the very landscape of the area owes its character to sheep. But Cotswold Woollen Weavers keeps the flag flying, producing quality clothes, on clattering old looms, to suit most tastes. The factory premises are an attractive old barn. All the processes of production can be watched and, while it is a serious business concern, the historical relevance of wool production is not overlooked, for there is a permanent exhibition devoted to sheep and wool. There are also a café, an art gallery and an excellent shop. Adjoining buildings contain more workshops devoted to other traditional crafts.

A short distance east of Filkins are some interesting little villages. The Norman south doorway of the church at Kencot dates back to the 12th century and is decorated with a carving of Sagittarius shooting an arrow into the mouth of a monster. The church at Alvescot, which is set in a quiet location to the north of the village, has a splendid 16th-century brass.

KELMSCOTT   MAP REF SU2499

The fame of this small village is inseparable from the 19th-century poet and artist, William Morris. On the façade of a terrace of cottages on the main street, there he is in carved relief seated in the shade of a tree, knapsack and hat at his side. Kelmscott Manor, on the edge of the village, was his home from 1871 until his death in 1896. He is buried in the local churchyard in a grave, designed by Philip Webb and modelled on a Viking tomb.

Kelmscott Manor (limited public opening) was built in the late 16th century. Morris only rented it but it now contains a fine collection of items associated with the man and with his craft, most notably those comparatively simple, domestic artefacts that he strove to see reinvigorated through the Arts and Crafts Movement. It also contains pictures by Rossetti and Burne-Jones. This village came to mean much to him, and he named his private printing press in London after it. He also wrote the following, sentimental lines:

'The wind's on the wold and the night is a-cold
And the Thames runs chill twixt mead and hill
But kind and dear is the old house here
And my heart is warm midst winter's harm.'

■ Insight

LORD OF THE MANOR

The influence of the Tame family and the proximity of the river led Henry VIII's librarian, John Leland, to observe: 'Fairforde never flourished afore ye Tames came to it'. Wool merchant John Tame, who built Fairford's church, became Fairford's lord of the manor. His son, Sir Edmund Tame, is responsible for St Peter's at Rendcomb, 5 miles (8km) north of Cirencester, where his initials can be found on some of the corbels and on old glass in a nave window. It is thought that the church tower at Barnsley was largely the result of his patronage.

LECHLADE MAP REF SU2199

Another town with the peculiar quality that derives more from its rivers, notably the Thames, than from the Cotswolds. In the Middle Ages it was on the Salt Way but Lechlade is very much a river town. At the confluence of three rivers – the Coln, the Leach and the Thames – it was at Lechlade that the stone quarried at Taynton was loaded on to wagons before setting out for London, to be used in the construction of the great St Paul's Cathedral. From 1789 the Thames was linked to the Severn via the Thames and Severn Canal (which started to the southeast at Inglesham, where the old round house, built for the canal lengthmen (who were responsible for the maintenance of certain lengths of the canal), still stands.

Inevitably, wherever there are rivers there are bridges. Just south of the town, the A361 crosses the Thames with the old tollbridge, the 18th-century Halfpenny (or Ha'penny) Bridge; while to the east the A417 crosses the Thames by means of the 13th-century St John Bridge where a statue of Father Thames presides close to the Thames' highest lock and from where there is a fine view of the town.

Lechlade is built about its Market Square, and its wool church. The square, and the streets that radiate from it – Burford Street, High Street and St John Street – are overlooked by a collection of fine 17th- to 19th-century buildings. The church, with its distinctive spire, dates from the late 15th century when it was built largely from the same quarries at Taynton that later provided

the stone for St Paul's. It contains an east window from 1510 and the brass of wool merchant, John Townsend, as well as a fine chancel roof. One balmy summer evening in 1815 the church inspired the Romantic poet Percy Shelley to write:

> 'Thou too, aerial pile! Whose pinnacles
> Point from one shrine like pyramids
> of fire'

The bustle of commercial river life has long gone from Lechlade, although pleasure craft still bring colour and movement to the river and it is possible to hire small boats from the boatyard near the Ha'penny Bridge. The walk along the Thames, southwest from the Ha'penny Bridge, is very enjoyable and at Inglesham there is the pretty church of St John the Baptist, 30ft (100m) from the river, which was saved from decay by William Morris.

Just to the southeast of Lechlade is Buscot Park, a handsome 18th-century house, with a well-known series of paintings by Burne-Jones in the saloon, and a trio of Rembrandts among many other works of art reflecting the taste of the 1st Lord Faringdon. The house is set in an attractive park close to the village of Buscot, with its interesting church, and 18th-century parsonage owned by the National Trust.

MINSTER LOVELL
MAP REF SP3111

Here is a small village of particular interest. It is, first of all, exceptionally pretty – a fine old bridge spans the

Windrush and the main street is lined with an even mixture of Cotswold stone and thatch. Enjoy an entertaining introduction to the village at the Minster Lovell Heritage Centre, just over half a mile (800m) away on the Burford Road.

You can park at the far end of the street and then walk down to the church. It used to be accompanied by a priory, but it was dissolved in 1414. The remaining church, dedicated to St Kenelm, is quite beautiful. Its beauty is less evident from the outside, but once you go in, the perfection of its design becomes obvious. It is welcoming and comforting, well-tended like a cared-for drawing room, yet uplifting and peaceful. Cruciform in shape, it was built in 1431 on the foundations of an earlier 12th-century church. It lacks only the warming colours of stained-glass windows and some of the other humanising features that have gone in the last few hundred years. But the font is original and the alabaster tomb is thought to belong to William, 7th Baron Lovell, who built the church.

Behind the church, on the banks of the Windrush, stands the romantic ruin of Minster Lovell Hall, which was built, like the church, by William Lovell. Originally a fortified manor house on a grand scale, it was sold to Sir Thomas Coke whose descendants dismantled it in 1747, the remains finding a less salubrious use as farm buildings until the 1930s. A short stroll from the Hall, across the field among other farm buildings and also open to the public, is the sturdy, round, medieval dovecote.

A short distance from Minster Lovell, and a pleasant walk along the river, is the pretty village of Crawley with a river bridge and an old blanket mill.

Just to the south of Minster Lovell lie the Charterville Allotments, the subject of a 19th-century social experiment. The 300 acres (121ha) were purchased by the Chartists and offered as smallholdings to poor families, along with £30 and a pig. The experiment failed but some of the cottages remain.

THE ROLLRIGHT STONES
MAP REF SP3031

These ancient monuments, on the side of the A3400 road between Shipston-on-Stour and Chipping Norton, not far from Long Compton, consist of two stone circles and a monolith.

The three elements of the Rollright Stones have each been given a name, the King's Men, the Whispering Knights and the King Stone, which derive from a legend explaining their origins. Long ago a band of soldiers met a witch who told them that if their leader were to take seven long strides and 'if Long Compton

---

thou canst see, King of England thou shall be'. The aspiring monarch risked all, saw nothing and was, along with his loyal followers, turned to stone. The Whispering Knights are the traitors who planned to overthrow the king once he became ruler of all England.

The facts are more banal. The 77 King's Men, 100 feet (30.8m) in diameter, and the King Stone, are said to date from 3000–2000 BC, during the Bronze Age; their purpose is uncertain. The Whispering Knights are believed to be the remains of a Neolithic long barrow. The Stones, which can be seen from the A3400, are open to the public, but parking is limited.

The village of Little Rollright has a fine 17th-century manor house and a handsome little church built in the Perpendicular style, which contains some magnificent 17th-century stone monuments. Great Rollright has fine views southwards over rolling countryside. Its historic buildings include the Norman church with its gargoyles and carved doorway. Close by is Wyatt's Tea Room, where organic food and plants are available.

Long Compton, strung out along the A3400 and not far from the Rollright Stones, is an attractive village with a handsome Perpendicular church, which you approach through a lychgate, thought to be a cottage with its lower floor removed.

The Rollright Stones are not far from the Jurassic Way, A long-distance footpath connecting Banbury and Stamford. It runs for 88 miles (142km) and follows the line of the Jurassic

■ Insight

A MACABRE LEGEND
Several legends attach themselves to Minster Lovell Hall. The strangest of all concerns Francis Lovell, a Yorkist, who fled after the Battle of Bosworth, returning in 1487 to champion the cause of the pretender, Lambert Simnel. Defeated at the Battle of Stoke, Lovell returned to the Hall and locked himself in a secret room, attended by a dog and a servant. Somehow, when the servant died, Lovell became trapped in the room and died there. In 1708, during work on the house, a skeleton was apparently discovered seated at a desk, with a dog at its feet.

limestone ridge passing through a wide variety of different landscapes. It links with the Macmillan Way which passes through Stow-on-the-Wold..

SHIPSTON-ON-STOUR
MAP REF SP2540

As its name implies, Shipston was for long an important sheep market town. After the demand for local wool began to decline in the 19th century the town continued to prosper thanks to the opening of a branch line in 1836 from the horse-drawn tramway linking Moreton-in-Marsh with Stratford-on-Avon. This line was converted to steam power in 1889. Before that it was an important stop for coaches, and many of the inns in the High Street date from that time.

Around Shipston there are a number of villages that are worth a visit. To the northwest is Ilmington, a delightful scattered village that has a fine manor house and a church that contains work

■ Visit

HOOK NORTON

Hook Norton, east of Great Rollright, is known these days, above all, for its beer. Brewed in a Victorian red-brick brewery, Hook Norton Ale is affectionately known as 'Hooky'. Brewery tours are run from their Visitor Centre, which is next door to the village museum. The village's former importance as an ironstone centre is evident from the remains of a huge railway viaduct across the valley.

■ Visit

TRAGIC VOYAGE

On the green of Shipton-under-Wychwood, close to the Shaven Crown, is a memorial of 1878 erected to 17 parishioners who died in a ship named the *Cospatrick* which caught fire off Cape Town in 1874 on its way to New Zealand. Tragically, of the 477 passengers presumably aiming to start a new life, only three survived.

by Robert Thompson, the celebrated early 20th-century furniture maker and craftsman whose signature was always a wooden mouse. To the north is the attractive village of Honington, which is approached by a minor road leading over a five-arched bridge.

Just north of Honington you can find the well-manicured village of Tredington complete with its parish church and fine 15th-century spire. In the porch floor there are the curious fossilised remains of a creature like an ichthyosaurus (a fish lizard). To the south of Shipston is Cherington with a good selection of attractive 18th- and 19th-century houses built of local stone.

SHIPTON-UNDER-WYCHWOOD   MAP REF SP2817

Formerly the neighbour of Bruern Abbey, and once the centre of the Wychwood Forest, Shipton is built about a large village green in the Evenlode Valley.

At the lower end of the green is St Mary's Church, begun at the end of the 13th century. A fine octagonal spire grows out of its tower, while within the church there is a 14th-century effigy of a woman and a delightful Tudor monument of a family group at prayer.

The apparently uniquely named Shaven Crown Hotel, a handsome stone building close to the green, can trace its history back to 1384 and was run at one time by the Cistercian monks of Bruern Abbey. Bruern was founded in the reign of King Stephen and dissolved in 1536 – nothing now remains. The Shaven Crown, however, once hosted the Fascist leader Oswald Mosley when he was arrested during the Second World War.

Of Wychwood Forest there is almost nothing left, although it once covered a large area between Stanton Harcourt and Taynton and a project is underway to restore some of its original landscape and habitats. It was much used by the Normans for hunting and was well known for its deer – indeed the citizens of Burford were entitled to hunt there. Most English kings up to Charles I hunted here. In later centuries many of the notable estate parks in the vicinity – Blenheim and Cornbury, for example – were carved out of it and in the centre of the remaining area of forest stands a National Nature Reserve which is just 2 miles (3.2km) east of Shipton.

Burford – a Classic Cotswold Town

Wonderful panoramas to the surrounding hills, a jewelled lake and sylvan splendour are some of the delights of this walk. St Oswald's Church, which you pass on the walk, was built on the site of a Roman villa. Near the altar is a mosaic floor, only discovered at the start of the 20th century. The nearby abandoned site of a medieval village might fire your imagination with images of everyday life in those days. Shortly after, you continue beside the delightful River Windrush valley into Burford.

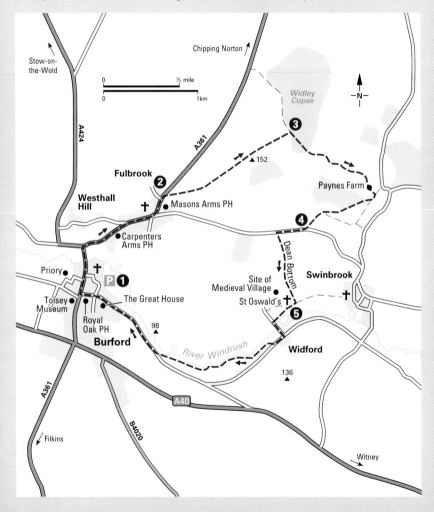

Route Directions

1 Head north along the High Street to the Windrush. Cross the river and turn right at the mini-roundabout towards Fulbrook. Pass the Carpenters Arms and continue along the road. Avoid a turning for Swinbrook and pass the Masons Arms. Keep ahead, passing Upper End on the left, and look for a footpath on the right.

2 Follow the steps cut into the side of the slope up to the field-edge and then swing right. Follow the boundary to a waymark just before a slope and curve left to cross the field. Go through a gap in the hedge on the far side and cross the field to an opening in the hedgerow. Cross the next field towards a curtain of woodland and make for a track.

3 Keep right and follow the track through the woodland. Break cover from the trees and pass a row of cottages. Continue down the track to Paynes Farm and, just beyond it, turn right to join a signposted right of way. Head for a gate and follow the unfenced track towards trees. Descend the slope to a gate and continue ahead between hedges up the hill to the road

4 Turn right and follow the road down into a dip. Swing left at the stile and sign for Widford and follow the grassy ride through verdant Dean Bottom. Make for a stile, turn right when you reach the T-junction and visit Widford's St Oswald's Church.

5 On leaving the church, veer right and follow the grassy track, passing a lake on the left. Turn left at the road, recross the Windrush and turn right at the junction. Keep to the road until you reach a footpath sign and stile on the right. Follow the riverside path across a series of stiles, to eventually reach the road. Turn right towards Burford, pass the Great House and the Royal Oak and return to the High Street.

Route facts

DISTANCE/TIME
5 miles (8km) 2h30

MAP OS Explorer OL45 The Cotswolds

START Burford: large car park to east of Windrush, near parish church; grid ref: SP 255123

TRACKS Field and riverside paths, tracks, country roads, 7 stiles

GETTING TO THE START
Burford stands by a crossroads of the A40, between Oxford and Cheltenham, and the A361 north from Swindon. The car park, from which the walk begins, is signed along Church Lane from the A361 in the town centre.

THE PUB The Swan, Swinbrook. Tel: 01993 822165

Beyond Chipping Norton

This route takes you from Chipping Norton to the Rollright Stones, a group of prehistoric megalithic monuments created from large natural boulders that overlook the rolling hills and valleys of the northeast Cotswolds.

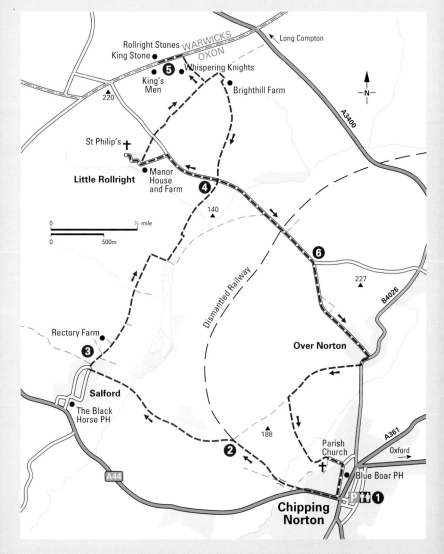

Route Directions

1 Follow the A44, New Street, downhill. Pass Penhurst School, then veer right through a kissing gate. Skirt the left-hand edge of the recreation ground and aim for a gate. Descend to a bridge, cross over, and, when the path forks, keep right. Go up the slope to a kissing gate. Cross a drive and continue to the next tarmac drive. Keep ahead to a stile and along the right-hand edge of a field. Make for gate and drop down to some double gates on the right.

2 Go through. Turn sharp left and walk towards Salford, keeping the hedge on the left. Continue into the village and soon turn right by some grass and a sign, 'Trout Lakes – Rectory Farm'.

3 Follow the track to a right-hand bend. Go straight ahead here, following the field edge. Make for a gate ahead and turn right in the next field. About 100yds (91m) before the field corner, turn left and follow the path across to an opening in the boundary. Veer left, then immediately right to skirt the field. Cross a little stream and maintain your direction in the next field to reach the road.

4 Turn left, then left again for Little Rollright. After visiting the church, retrace your steps to the D'Arcy Dalton Way on the left. Follow the path up the field slope to the road. Cross over and continue on the way between fields. Head for some trees and approach a stile. Don't cross it; instead, turn left and skirt the field, passing close to the Whispering Knights.

5 On reaching the road, turn left and visit the site of the Rollright Stones. Return to the Whispering Knights, head down the field to the stile and cross it to an immediate second stile. Walk ahead along a grassy path and turn right at the next stile towards Brighthill Farm. Pass alongside the buildings to a stile, head diagonally right down the field to a double stile, keep the boundary on your right and head for a galvanised gate in the bottom right corner of the field. Make for the bottom right corner of the next field, go through a gate and skirt the field, turning left at the road.

6 Keep right at the next fork and head towards the village of Over Norton. Walk through the village to the T-junction. Turn right and when the road swings to the left by Cleeves Corner, join a track signposted 'Salford'. When the hedges on the left give way, look for a waymark on the left. Follow the path down the slope, make for two kissing gates and then follow the path alongside a stone wall to reach the parish church. Join Church Lane and follow it as far as the T-junction. Turn right and return to the town centre.

Route facts

DISTANCE/TIME
8 miles (12.9km) 4h

MAP OS Explorer 191 Banbury, Bicester & Chipping Norton

START The walk begins from a long-stay car park signed left off the A44, opposite the entrance to the supermarket car park; grid ref: SP 313271

TRACKS Field paths, tracks, country roads, 7 stiles

GETTING TO THE START Chipping Norton is 12 miles (19.3km) southwest of Banbury by the junction of the A361 and A44.

THE PUB The Chequers, Chipping Norton. Tel: 01608 644717; www.chequers-pub.com

❶ This long walk is suitable for fitter, older families

THE WINDRUSH VALLEY

The Windrush rises near Taddington, south of Snowshill, and wanders through several villages. Beyond Bourton it widens as it approaches the Thames and continues through a number of villages to the north of the A40 to join the Thames. A pleasant walk, the Windrush Way, goes from Winchcombe to Bourton-on-the-Water.

Sherborne, on a tributary of the Windrush, has been for centuries part of the Sherborne estate; before that the land was owned by the Abbots of Winchcombe, whose sheep were sheared on the banks of the river every summer. Sherborne House, allegedly haunted by its former owner, John 'Crump' Dutton, the Royalist hunchback, was rebuilt in the 19th century. Occupied by the military during the Second World War, it then became a boarding school. It now belongs to the National Trust and, although it is not open to the public, there are waymarked walks through the woods and parkland. Lodge Park, an elaborate grandstand for deer-coursing in the 17th century, is open to the public.

The next village to the east is Windrush with a church topped by a fine Perpendicular tower and a magnificent Norman south doorway surrounded by beakheads, bird-like grotesques of mysterious origin. Then come the Barringtons, first Little, then Great, once renowned for their stone quarries and the local families of masons, the Kempsters and the Strongs, who worked them. No evidence remains of the old subterranean quarries and Little Barrington is a quiet village, its cottages very prettily clustered about its village green. The Fox Inn, nearby, is by a bridge over the river, built by local master mason Thomas Strong, principal contractor of St Paul's and regarded by Christopher Wren as the leading builder of the day. Great Barrington, to the north, has a Norman church with some fine monuments by the 18th-century sculptor Joseph Nollekens, while the country house and landscaped gardens of Barrington Park are to the east of it.

East of Great Barrington lies Taynton, another village that once supplied London and Oxford with its famous prime building stone – taken from open-cast quarries, it was transported overland to Lechlade and thence by barge to London. Beyond it is Burford and then Widford church, the poignant remains of a once thriving village that simply disappeared, probably as a result of the plague. The 13th-century church, built on the site of a Roman villa, stands small and solitary on a raised mound overlooking the river, and is worth a look for its box pews, and the wall paintings that date from the 14th century.

A short way from Widford is Swinbrook, a village associated with the Mitford family, particularly five of Lord Redesdale's daughters, Nancy, Diana, Unity, Jessica and Deborah. Unity became a close friend of Adolf Hitler,

Diana married the British fascist leader, Sir Oswald Moseley, Deborah became the Duchess of Devonshire, while Nancy and Jessica became well-known writers. Nancy, Pamela, Diana and Unity are buried in the graveyard of the church, which contains the wonderful triple-decker monument to the Fettiplace family who once owned a mansion here. Across the river to the southeast is Asthall, a charming village with a fine Elizabethan manor. Exhibitions of stone sculpture are held in the gardens, for a short period every other summer.

WITNEY MAP REF SP3510

Another Windrush town, Witney remains famous for its blankets, the production of which somehow managed to survive the collapse of the Cotswold woollen industry after the Industrial Revolution. The Market Square is the centre of the town and contains an unusual Butter Cross, refurbished in the 19th century, and the 17th-century Town Hall. Beyond, near a green, is the 13th-century church, complete with its massive tower, and a fine collection of houses that date from the 17th and 18th centuries. The town's museum is in Gloucester Court Mews in the High Street. Also in the High Street you will see the Blanket Hall, built in 1721 by the Company of Blanket Weavers, a group of prosperous weavers who were granted their charter in 1711.

Just to the southeast of Witney, and well-signposted on the A40, is the Cogges Manor Farm Museum, reflecting farming life in Victorian times. Among the machinery and livestock, you will find a working kitchen and dairy.

■ Visit

WIDFORD CHURCH

This isolated church at Widford is of mainly 13th-century origin and has some interesting wall paintings that date from the 14th century. The tiny church takes its name from St Oswald, the Saxon King of Northumbria who was killed in battle in AD 642 by Penda of Mercia. It is thought that the church owes its precise location to the fact that the saint's body was rested here on its way to burial at Gloucester.

WOODSTOCK MAP REF SP4416

Woodstock is a small town of some charm, just to the north of Oxford, most famous as the home of the Churchill family, whose ancestral home is Blenheim Palace. It has enjoyed royal patronage since Henry I built a park and hunting lodge here in the 12th century, which his grandson, Henry II, preferred to use to entertain his mistress, the fair Rosamund. The lodge became a palace and the town grew around it. The medieval author of *The Canterbury Tales* and *Troilus and Criseyde*, Geoffrey Chaucer, may have lived in Woodstock for some years, while in later centuries the town was noted for its glove-making.

Woodstock Palace was destroyed during the Civil War and Blenheim Palace was started in 1705 as a gift to John Churchill, 1st Duke of Marlborough after his success against the French at the Battle of Blenheim.

Designed by John Vanbrugh, it is perhaps the greatest palace in England, its Baroque extravagance brilliantly humanised by the beauty of the 2,000-acre (810ha) park, landscaped by 'Capability' Brown. The beauty of the relationship between the palace and its grounds can best be appreciated by walking from the town and entering the park through Nicholas Hawksmoor's Triumphal Arch, or the Woodstock Gate, just off Park Street. Merely to walk around the palace, cross the Grand Bridge and explore the views as you walk to the Column of Victory, is

Activity

PALATIAL PLAYGROUND

The grounds of Blenheim offer other distractions – there is a butterfly house and a children's playground and you can lose yourself in the Marlborough Maze. The park is also the venue for events such as craft fairs, horse trials and even jousting, throughout the year.

Insight

A DEMANDING EMPLOYER

A prodigious display of ill feeling, in keeping with the magnitude of the undertaking, sadly accompanied the construction of Blenheim Palace. The design is the work of Sir John Vanbrugh (who also built Castle Howard in Yorkshire) but with Sarah Jennings, the wife of the Duke of Marlborough, he found himself in the hands of a demanding employer. Her capricious nature finally led him to resign the commission in 1716, fortunately after most of the work had been accomplished. Although Nicholas Hawksmoor oversaw the final construction, it was, however, largely the Duchess' tenacity that ensured completion of the building after the death of her husband – not only did she find the money when Queen Anne's government failed to stump up all the promised funds, she was also responsible for much of the interior design.

breathtaking, but you can also enjoy the rose garden and the world's largest symbolic hedge maze.

The palace itself is replete with gilt and grandeur – carvings by Grinling Gibbons, Flemish tapestries illustrating the martial valour of the duke, and a fine collection of paintings. In the Great Hall is the magnificent ceiling painted by Sir James Thornhill, while the Long Library is one of the longest single rooms in Britain. The first duke and duchess are buried in the chapel, which was built by Hawksmoor in 1731. The room where Sir Winston Churchill was born is the focal point of an exhibition devoted to his life.

The town of Woodstock itself is worthy of some exploration. The streets that cluster around the 18th-century Town Hall are lined with a fine assortment of houses and inns from the 17th and 18th centuries. The most famous is the ivy-clad Bear Hotel, which dates back to the 13th century. The Parish Church of St Mary Magdalen is set in a charming churchyard and is surmounted by a classical tower of 1785. The original Norman south doorway is particularly fine.

Opposite the church, in Park Street, is Fletcher's House. Originally built for a 17th-century merchant, it now houses the Oxfordshire Museum, with galleries and exhibitions about the history and traditions of Oxfordshire covering three floors. The museum has a convenient small café and bookshop. The elegant townhouse also has pleasant gardens. The town stocks are preserved at the museum entrance.

■ TOURIST INFORMATION CENTRES

Burford
The Brewery, Sheep Street.
Tel: 01993 823558

Chipping Norton
The Guildhall, Goddards Lane. Tel: 01993 861326

Witney
Town Hall, Market Square.
Tel: 01993 775802

Woodstock
Oxfordshire Museum, Park Street. Tel: 01993 813276

■ PLACES OF INTEREST

Asthall Manor
Tel: 01993 824319;
www.onformsculpture.co.uk

Blenheim Palace
Woodstock.
Tel: 0800 849 6500;
www.blenheimpalace.com

Chipping Norton Museum
High Street, Chipping Norton.
Tel: 01608 641712

Churchill and Sarsden Heritage Centre
Churchill Old Church, Hastings Hill, Churchill.
Tel: 01608 658603

Cogges Manor Farm Museum
Church Lane, Witney.
Tel: 01993 772602;
www.cogges.org

Cotswold Wildlife Park and Gardens
Burford. Tel: 01993 823006;
www.cotswoldwildlifepark.co.uk

Hook Norton Brewery Visitor Centre
Brewery Lane, Hook Norton.
Tel: 01608 730384; www.hooknortonbrewery.co.uk

Kelmscott Manor
Kelmscott. Tel: 01367 252486;
www.kelmscottmanor.org.uk

Minster Lovell Hall and Dovecote
Minster Lovell.
Tel: 0870 333 1181;
www.english-heritage.org.uk
Free.

Minster Lovell Heritage Centre
130 Burford Road, Minster Lovell. Tel: 01993 775262;
www.minsterlovell.com

North Leigh Roman Villa
North Leigh.
www.english-heritage.org.uk
Free.

Oxfordshire Museum
Fletcher's House,
Park Street, Woodstock.
Tel: 01993 811456;
www.oxfordshire.gov.uk

Tolsey Museum
High Street, Burford.
Tel: 01993 822178; www.tolseymuseumburford.com

Witney and District Museum
Gloucester Court Mews,
High Street, Witney.
Tel: 01993 775915

■ SHOPPING

Chipping Norton
Farmers' Market, third Sat, Market Square.

Witney
Farmers' Market, third Wed, Market Place.

LOCAL SPECIALITIES
Wool
Cotswold Woollen Weavers, Filkins. Tel: 01367 860491;
www.naturalbest.co.uk

■ PERFORMING ARTS

Chipping Norton Theatre
Spring Street, Chipping
Norton. Tel: 01608 642350;
www.chippingnortontheatre.co.uk

■ OUTDOOR ACTIVITIES

HORSE-RIDING
Nether Westcote
Overdale Equestrian Centre.
Tel: 01993 832520

■ ANNUAL EVENTS & CUSTOMS

Bledington
Music Festival, Jun.

Blenheim
International Horse Trials, Sep.

Burford
Annual Levellers Day, May.

Chadlington
International Music Festival, Jun.

Chipping Norton
Music Festival, Mar.
Jazz Festival, Sep.

Fairford
Royal International Air Tattoo, Jul.

THE BEAR H...
Morning Coff...
with Home made B...
& Pastries

Traditional En...
Afternoon T...

Sandwiches & L...
served in our...
all da...

Restaurant...
Monday to...
2.30pm Saturd...

Tea Rooms

Huffkins
98 High Street, Burford
OX18 4QF
Tel: 01993 822126;
www.huffkins.com
A wonderful range of freshly
made speciality bread and
cakes is on sale here, with
tempting sandwiches and
home-made soup as well.
In addition to the tea room,
there is a well-stocked shop.

Wyatt's Tea Room
Hill Barn Farm,
Great Rollright,
Nr Chipping Norton OX7 5SH
Tel: 01608 684835
Part of a popular farm shop,
this spacious and very clean
tea room is justifiably
popular. Anything from light
lunches to mouth-watering
teas can be enjoyed
throughout the year.

Daylesford Organic
Daylesford,
Nr Kingham GL56 0YG
Tel: 01608 731700;
www.daylesfordorganic.com
Enjoy organic handmade
bread and pastries and
traditional afternoon tea at
this beautifully designed café.
There's also a farm shop,and
a cookery and farm school.
There's even a yoga studio
with a lovely rural view.

Harriet's
20 High Street,
Woodstock OX20 1TF
Tel: 01993 811231
The finest continental-style
croissants, cakes and
patisseries are made here
by a Frenchman, and most
of the other food, such as
the clotted cream and the
honey, is sourced from
local producers.

Pubs

The Bull Inn
Sheep Street,
Charlbury OX7 3RR
Tel: 01608 810689;
www.bullinn-charlbury.com
Low beams, inglenook
fireplaces and scrubbed
wood floors create the
appropriate atmosphere in
this 16th-century coaching
inn. Outside, the vine-covered
terrace is the ideal place to
enjoy the sunshine.

The Crown Inn
Mill Lane, Church Enstone
OX7 4NN
Tel: 01608 677262
Run by an award-winning
chef, this 17th-century stone
inn is comfortable and
welcoming. They specialise in
fresh fish; all the food comes
from local suppliers and is
delicious. There is also a
picturesque cottage garden.

Swan at Southrop
Southrop GL7 3NU
Tel: 01367 850205;
www.theswanatsouthrop.co.uk
It is worth going out of your
way to find this handsome
gastropub. It is bright and
comfortable inside and the
food, sourced locally where
possible, is first class and
provided by a top chef who
has moved from London.

The Fox
Great Barrington,
Nr Burford OX18 4TB
Tel: 01451 844385;
www.foxinnbarrington.com
Idyllically situated on the
banks of the River Windrush,
this is a perfect place to
unwind. The pretty patio and
beer garden look down on the
river, while inside there are
old beams and real fires.
There is an inventive menu
and good local beers.

The Fox and Hounds Inn
Great Wolford CV36 5NQ
Tel: 01608 674220;
www.thefoxandhoundsinn.com
A really unspoiled pub in the
northern Cotswolds,
surrounded by wonderful
countryside.The food here is
very good, and there is a huge
selection of whiskies.

■ OTHER INFORMATION

English Heritage

29 Queen Square, Bristol, BS1 4ND.
Tel: 0117 975 0700;
www.english-heritage.org.uk

National Trust

Wessex Region, Eastleigh Court, Bishopstrow, Warminster, BA12 9HW.
Tel: 01985 843624;
www.nationaltrust.org.uk

Wildlife Trust

Tel: 01452 383333
www.gloucestershirewildlife trust.co.uk

Parking

Park with care in small villages which have no car parks and take care not to block driveways or field entrances. If you park on the road, allow room for vehicles, including lorries, to pass.

Places of interest

There will be an admission charge unless otherwise stated. We give details of just some of the places to visit within the area covered by this guide. Further information can be obtained from local tourist information centres or the internet.

Weather Call

For details of weather conditions in Wiltshire, Gloucestershire and Avon.
Tel: 09068 500 405

Cycling

The website for the Cotswold District Council (www.cotswold.gov.uk) has downloadable cycling routes on quiet lanes and farm tracks and also has details on where to hire bikes. The book *Pub Walks & Cycle Rides the Cotswolds*, from AA Publishing, has 40 walks and cycle rides, with each route mapped.

Walking

For further information on the 100-mile (161km) long Cotswold Way National Trail, see www.nationaltrail.co.uk/Cotswold/

Birdwatching

For information on the Wildfowl & Wetlands Trust centre at Slimbridge in Gloucestershire, see www.wwt.org.uk/visit/slimbridge/

Public Transport

A great website for public transport is the Cotswolds Area of Outstanding Natural Beauty site, www.cotswoldsaonb.com. Search for 'Transport' and you'll find bus and train timetables for each area of the Cotswolds.

Fishing

The Cotswold Water Park in South Cerney has numerous lakes where you can go fishing. See the website at www.waterpark.org/leisure/angling.html

■ ORDNANCE SURVEY MAPS

NORTHERN COTSWOLDS

Landranger 1:50,000;
Sheets 150, 151, 163.
Outdoor Leisure 1:25,000;
Sheet 45

SEVERN VALE

Landranger 1:50,000;
Sheets 150, 162, 172.

SOUTHERN COTSWOLDS

Explorer 1:25,000;
Sheets 155, 167, 168, 169, 179.
Landranger 1: 50,000;
Sheets 162, 163, 172, 173.

EASTERN COTSWOLDS

Explorer 1:25,000 Sheet 180.
Landranger 1: 50,000 Sheets 151, 163, 164. Outdoor Leisure 1:25,000 Sheet 45.

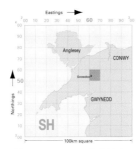

The National Grid system covers Great Britain with an imaginary network of grid squares. Each is 100km square in area and is given a unique alphabetic reference, as shown in the diagram above.

These squares are sub-divided into one hundred 10km squares, identified by vertical lines (eastings) and horizontal lines (northings). The reference for the square a feature is located within is made by adding the numbers of the two lines which cross in the bottom left corner of that square to the alphabetic reference (ignoring the small figures). The easting is quoted first. For example, SH6050.

For a 2-figure reference, the zeros are omitted, giving just SH65. In this book, we use 4-figure references, which allow us to pinpoint the feature more accurately by dividing the 10km square into one hundred 1km squares. These squares are not actually printed on the road atlas but are estimated by eye. The same process is carried out as before, giving an enhanced reference of SH6154.

Key to Atlas

Motorway with number	Toll	Abbey, cathedral or priory		National Trust for Scotland property	NTS
Motorway service area	Road underconstruction	Aquarium		Nature reserve	
Motorway toll	Narrow Primary route with passing places	Castle		Other place of interest	
Motorway junction with and without number	Steep gradient	Cave		Park and Ride location	P+R
Restricted motorway junctions	Railway station and level crossing	Country park		Picnic site	
Motorway and junction under construction	Tourist railway	County cricket ground		Steam centre	
Primary route single/dual carriageway	National trail	Farm or animal centre		Ski slope natural	
Primary route destinations	Forest drive	Garden		Ski slope artifical	
Roundabout	Heritage coast	Golf course		Tourist Information Centre	
Distance in miles between symbols	Ferry route	Historic house		Viewpoint	
Other A Road single/dual carriageway	Walk start point	Horse racing		Visitor or heritage centre	
		Motor racing			
B road single/dual carriageway	Cycle start point	Museum		Zoological or wildlife collection	
Unclassified road single/dual carriageway	Tour start point	Airport		Forest Park	
		Heliport		National Park (England & Wales)	
Road tunnel		Windmill			
		National Trust property	NT	National Scenic Area (Scotland)	

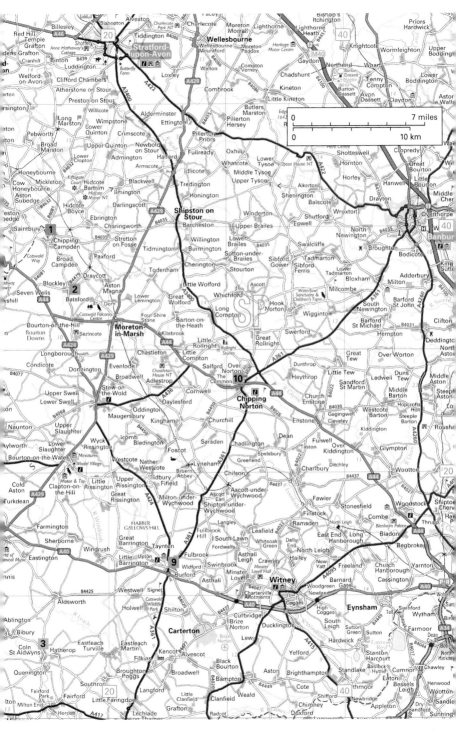

The Automobile Association would like to thank the following photographers and companies for their assistance in the preparation of this book. Abbreviations for the picture credits are as follows – (t) top; (b) bottom; (c) centre; (l) left; (r) right; (AA) AA World Travel Library

1 AA/H Palmer; 4/5 AA/F Stephenson; 8t AA/ D Hall; 8b AA/ D Hall; 9 AA/D Hall; 10t AA/D Hall; 10b AA/H Palmer; 11t AA/H Palmer; 11b AA/S Day; 13 AA/S Day; 14tl AA/D Hall; 14tr AA/D Hall; 14b AA/M Birkitt; 18bl AA/D Hall; 18br AA/D Hall; 19 AA/D Hall; 21t AA/S Day; 21b AA/S Day; 22 AA/S Day; 23t AA/H Palmer; 23b AA/S Day; 29 AA/D Hall; 33 AA/S Day; 41 AA/D Hall; 50 AA/D Hall; 52bl AA/H Palmer; 52br AA/D Hall; 53 AA/D Hall; 55t AA/S Day; 55b AA/C Jones; 56 AA/D Hall; 57t AA/ADCTAC©Liquid Light/Alamy; 57b AA/E Meacher; 60 AA/H Palmer; 67 AA/T Souter; 70 AA/H Palmer; 74 AA/D Hall; 78 AA/H Palmer; 80bl AA/D Hall; 80br AA/D Hall; 81 AA/D Hall; 83tl AA/D Hall; 83tr AA; 83b AA/D Hall; 84 AA/S Day; 85t AA/S and O Mathews; 85c AA/D Hall; 85b AA/K Doran; 89 AA/C Jones; 94 AA/K Doran; 103 AA/D Hall; 106 AA/D Hall; 111 AA/D Hall; 118 AA/D Hall; 120l AA/S Day; 120r AA/S Day; 121 AA/S Day; 123tl AA/D Hall; 123tr AA/S Day; 123b AA/D Hall; 124 AA/C Jones; 125t AA/S Day; 125b AA/R Rainford; 129 AA/D Hall; 134©Nick Turner/Alamy; 139 AA/V Greaves; 147 AA/D Hall; 148 AA/K Doran; 150 AA/D Hall.

Every effort has been made to trace the copyright holders, and we apologise in advance for any accidental errors. We would be happy to apply the corrections in the following edition of this publication.